Modern Romance

Neurobiology to the Rescue

The
Neuroscience
Of
Dating

By Heidi Crockett

Modern Romance Neurobiology to the Rescue

The Neuroscience of Dating

Copyright © 2017 Heidi Crockett

All rights reserved. No part of this book may be reproduced in any form or by any electronic or mechanical means, including information storage and retrieval systems, without permission in writing from the author. For information, contact HeidiCrockett@gmail.com.

The content of this book is for general instruction only. Each person's physical, mental, and emotional condition is unique. The instruction in this book is not intended to replace or interrupt the reader's relationship with a physician or other professional. Please consult your doctor for matters pertaining to your specific health.

To contact the author, visit

www.RedLightHeidi.com

ISBN: 0996232230
ISBN-13: 978-0-9962322-3-4

Dynamic Learning
314 Shore Dr. E.
Oldsmar, FL 34677-3916

Published in the United States by Dynamic Learning

DEDICATION

This book is dedicated to the transformative power of Couple Love, also called Couple Enlightenment.

If you seek to be a couple and circulate pure love, may you find it, heal each other with it, and use that love to heal the world.

CONTENTS

	Introduction	1
1	Clarity	12
2	Clarity and the River of Brain Integration	18
3	Fastly Flowing Down the River	35
4	Your 1-2-3 Dating Tips	43
5	Riverbank of Chaos Mistakes	75
6	Dishonesty from Within	90
7	Dishonesty from Others	98
8	Riverbank of Rigidity Mistakes	121
9	Understanding the River and Letting Go	135
10	Dopamine as the Engine of Your Boat	151
11	Why You Are Alive	162
12	Bringing It All Together	175
	Glossary, Appendices, Index	178

ACKNOWLEDGMENTS

I want to thank all the scientists for their hard work and decades of research collecting data on the brain and relationships especially Dr. Dan Siegel and the field of Interpersonal Neurobiology. Although I am a licensed psychotherapist, I have no formal training in neuroscience. I appreciate my beta readers for your useful feedback. Thank you to all my teachers for inspiring and encouraging me. Thank you to Sallie Foley and all the sexuality educators at the University of Michigan's Sexual Health Program. Finally, many thanks to my family and friends for your nourishing love and support.

THE NEUROSCIENCE OF DATING

INTRODUCTION

As you'll read from my dating stories in this book, I wanted some wild times and fun after my husband passed away. Whether your kids are starting kindergarten or you just finished legal paperwork on a nasty divorce, **life cycles us through difficult and fun times**. Regardless of where you are, I encourage you to be brave and start your dating journey **today**, taking into account whatever makes up your special life circumstances.

Looking around at the world in 2017, I would say that it's messy here. It is amazing, messy, difficult, and stress-inducing. Guess what? Dating is going to be like that too. I bet that your life is so busy that it can be hard to find free time. **And when you finally have some down time, you probably want life to be easy and fun.** This book takes evidence-based research from relational neuroscience and applies it to dating, so that you can save time, and you can have more fun!

On my dating journey, I did everything wrong, and I certainly didn't know or apply the principles in this book. I used my real name, I wasn't mindful about media, and I wasn't strict about dating safety when meeting people. I will say that I was lucky early on, and my advice is never to depend on luck.

What did I do right? I had fun! I discovered new things like TPE (total power exchange), butt plugs, role play, sexting, and talking dirty. How many people are curious about Who They Are and what they want sexually but are afraid to explore at the same time? I encourage you to apply this principle of brain integration: **don't let fear control you as you make smart, safe choices**. Fun is possible. Fun is when you are expressing and being yourself flowing down the river and everyone is safe and happy.

The problem for me in trying to explore and understand my sexual identity was that it seemed like millions of vultures were circling me. Sexual energy can be like a sugar addiction. Some people crave it and will go to extreme measures to get it. (Have you seen the "Jimmy Kimmel I Told My Kids I Ate All Their Halloween Candy" videos? Look at how those kids have extreme emotional responses when their candy is taken away and know that those same deep cravings and emotions happen in adults.)

I only went so far with my wild girl side because I had fear and anxiety. I feel lucky that I had the wherewithal to protect myself and set boundaries. This is dangerous, serious stuff that I write about here. Sex is so powerful it can create human life, yet there is a dark side to it, including forced pornography and sex trafficking. My intention in writing about it is to give a middle-of-the-road view. Times are changing, like fashion trends in girls' hemlines, and things like role play and spanking are considered quite vanilla and mainstream.

Certain conservatives think that sexual exploration should be curtailed and sex should only occur in the bedroom of a heterosexual, married couple. Then there is the liberal view that as long as sex acts are legal, everyone is consenting, and no one is getting hurt (unless they want to get hurt), anything can go.

I found I wanted to be liberal minded (hip, open, and someone who fit-in), but I had this gut feeling that sexuality was sacred and I needed to be careful about it. It was like I was offered the choice of the Riverbank of Conservative and the Riverbank of Liberal. I didn't identify with either riverbank. I had to find my own River of Sex Integration.

This book is written with the assumption that the reader wants one long-term life partner, but the principles here apply to whatever type of relationships or partners you seek. I want to stress that what you desire at one point in time can evolve. One example of this is how the desire for intimacy increases with age. So, my hope is that by applying the principles in this book, you will find the love you seek. Maybe you will also learn some valuable neuroscience tools and life skills along the way.

To help you with some of the fancier neurobiological terms, I have them in highlighted gray and defined them in the glossary.

THINGS I LEARNED ALONG THE WAY

1. I wish that I had known that extreme emotions even the thrill of sexual excitement can be red

flags that I am falling off my FASTly (I'll explain soon) flowing river.

2. Excitement is vital, as are other forms of pleasure like having someone's arms wrapped around me and having a trusted friend be there for me while I cry.

3. Some people have very different values from mine, including feeling that dishonesty with sex is acceptable. These values are often skillfully covered up (like by being hidden behind some sob story to tug at your emotions and turn your eyes and ears away from the reality of their behavior) because the person already knows that many people won't be OK with their values. (In other words, the person will be dishonest in getting sex **with you** because their values are that dishonesty and sex are OK.)

4. Sexual energy is the most sacred and powerful form of energy on the planet.

5. The mind is the most powerful and erotic tool for sex.

6. If anyone poo-poos the sacredness that you feel toward sexual energy, they are either triggered because of their issues or trying to manipulate you. I would choose to distance myself from someone who is responding in either fashion. Ultimately, you're seeking respect in a relationship, and these two responses are not respectful.

7. In the world of fantasy, being seen as an object (like with role play) can be a turn-on. In everyday plain-Jane life, the same behavior is anything but exciting. Discerning the difference between these two and making appropriate decisions require good emotional and erotic intelligence.

ADVICE FOR THE FUTURE

1. Lack of honesty is a **huge** red flag in relationships. **Run away** the minute that you find

out you have been seriously lied to. Even if you come back to the person, my recommendation is to give yourself **one month** in contemplation if you discover a major lie. If you **must** meet up with the person during this month, do it only in a safe space, which I recommend be an office with a counselor present. This month away is vital to your recovery of Self, regardless of whether you stay with the person who lied or not. When you are lied to, something is taken away. To reclaim what was lost takes times; it can't be magically whipped back with shallow forgiveness or some extreme rage or jealousy.

2. Most people are fine. The majority of screening tips in this book are more to find your perfect match and less about the fear of dangerous people.

3. Forgive yourself and forgive others for mistakes. Take responsibility for the good and bad outcomes of your actions. Learn from your mistakes.

4. Use one of the nine functions of the prefrontal cortex, insight, to better understand where and why there are guilt, fear, and shame in your life. Decide what these emotions mean to you as an adult. The brain changes each time we revisit a thought. Because of neurogenesis and neuroplasticity, we can think new thoughts and reframe old feelings. Doing this will enable you to respond instead of to react out of guilt, fear, or shame.

5. Question what you have been taught about sex. Question your beliefs around sex. Where did these teachings and your beliefs come from? Was there an agenda from the teacher? Does capitalism have an agenda in encouraging rampant pleasure seeking? If you experience uncertainty while questioning, protect yourself from manipulation. Whenever uncertain, err on the side of caution. **Your safety at all times is the highest priority**.

6. Just because someone has a strong opinion about something doesn't mean they are right; all you know is that they are pushy in that moment. And if someone is deeply sure about a belief, why do they need to prove it to anyone? Their being pushy is a red flag that they are probably wrong in some way.

7. Cultivate relationships that make you feel alive and grow you into your best version of yourself. Seek mentors who are inspiring people to you. Seek quality, not quantity in relationships.

8. Seek relationships where you are known and understood (and where you know and understand the other person). If people assume you are one fixed way and talk mostly about themselves when you are together, they are probably energy vampires. Look for relationships with attuned communication and give and take. Look for relationships where the other person seems like an unchartered universe with endless possibilities. When we are in the prefrontal

cortex, we tap into a nearly limitless capacity for attuned communication, for insight and empathy. When we are in fear in the limbic brain, judging people and seeing them as "other," as objects to acquire or reject, life feels colder and flatter and more isolating and war-like.

9. Life is too short to fake nice and pretend. Save time for everyone and learn to say no in a timely, loving, and firm fashion.

1 CLARITY

"Hope for love, pray for love, wish for love, dream for love…but don't put your life on hold waiting for love."
—Mandy Hale

Imagine this: a feeling of contentment and timelessness whenever you are with your (future) partner, the near-constant desire to touch, to be near, or to hold each other close because it feels so good, and you both never had **this** before, and you want to breathe it in. It's not just one night or one week or one month, but years and years pass, and you continue to feel close, circulating love, passion and compassion between you.

That paragraph could be **you** and the person who is

waiting to meet you.

Now if reading that felt like cheese-y times 1 million, maybe it'll help to know that I would have disdained it seven years ago. So, if you couldn't stand the start of this book, but you're willing to stick it out a bit longer, we'll go back to the fall of 2009 when I was in what I called my "Eat sh*t and die" phase after my husband died.

Well, before 2009, imagine a twenty-something college grad suffering from what I now call Naïve Disorder. No matter her circumstances she is happy and trusts people way too much, even when she is assaulted by a roommate with a resulting severe back injury. Even when dreaming her boyfriend is cheating on her, asking him about it, and his denying it. Then when they meet up, he tells her that he cheated on her, **and** she stays with him until he dumps her six months later **after the assault**. Even when her best girlfriend from out of town moves into her apartment and

immediately hooks up with the guy she's dating. And there are other stories like this. When she met her husband-to-be, and they found out he had a tumor the size of a baseball in his head three weeks into dating, she was like, "We can beat this!"

That was me in my twenties.

Fast-forward to October of 2009. My husband, Roger, had recently passed away after three incredibly awesome and terrible years with his brain tumor. In my barren landscape of grief, I fixate on the saving grace of pleasure. If someone reading this has problems with that, sue me.

I'm on a naughty website; it's fetlife or collarspace. I'm chatting with guys who tell me they are experienced Doms (dominants) and **they know how to take control.** I love it! I buy it hook, line, and sinker. I just want to be told what to do, I don't want to be in control of anyone's medical appointments or food intake or finances. **My first piece of advice is if it sounds too good to be true, it probably is.** (But I want to believe the fantasy so badly! I don't want things like rational judgment to get in my way!)

The most seductive men chatting with me had years, even decades of training to be that way. It is the same with online profiles: if someone looks perfect, if they say the right things, if they woo you exactly the way you always wanted to be wooed, **these are probably red flags.** Think, "Swiss cheese! I've got to find me those holes."

So, the first ingredient in a recipe for dating success is Clarity, which means:

1. Knowing Who You Are
2. Knowing what you seek in a partner

I **knew** who I was in October of 2009: I was submissive! It was so delightfully and deceptively simple: at the snap of someone's fingers I was a submissive, and all my worries melted away.

I needed fantasy to help rebuild my life and identity. My Clarity at that time was wanting sexual exploration and (safely) trying new things.

What is your Clarity? Maybe your ideal relationship looks and feels very different from how this chapter started. Whatever version of pure love that you seek, I hope the principles in this book help you to find it.

SUMMARY

To date successfully, it's important to have Clarity. Clarity is knowing Who You Are and knowing what you seek in a partner.

QUESTIONS

1. Take some time to write down some **essential** components that make up **you**. What are your passions in life? What do you want to learn more about? What are your dreams for your future?

   _____
   _____
   _____
   _____
   _____
   _____
   _____

2. After your write about yourself, write about what you imagine your future significant other to be like. How might what you plan to accomplish in life intersect with the aspirations of your future partner?

   _____
   _____
   _____
   _____
   _____

2 CLARITY AND THE RIVER OF BRAIN INTEGRATION

Why search for love? Why spend endless hours on dates or staring at a computer screen reading profiles of people who might not be real or who are certainly lying about something you are reading? Well, you are going to have to answer those questions, again and again.

Only you know your innermost longings. Only you know if your desires are coming from a place of imbalance and neediness versus a quiet knowing that there is something important out there that you must find. If you seek Couple Love, it is like the Holy Grail. Know that **it**

does exist. If you crave it, there must be some deeper reason inside why you want it. I'm suggesting you take a step back and explore using your prefrontal cortex, the part of your brain that thinks about thinking, and ask yourself these questions.

As mentioned in Chapter 1, Clarity is the first ingredient in a recipe for love success, and it's certainly **not** going to come from reading a book.

CLARITY

Using the River of Brain Integration,[i] Clarity would be represented by the figure of **you** steering your boat down the river (see picture). On either side of this river are the riverbanks of Rigidity and Chaos.

Warning! The next few pages go into more brain science terms to lay the foundation for a discussion on how neurobiology can help in dating. Feel free to skip this if it's too science-y and instead read the Summary on page 34.

WHAT IS CLARITY AND WHERE DOES CLARITY COME FROM?

Clarity comes from that search for meaning that is deeply personal. In my experience, clarity comes from self-understanding. In neuroscience, self-understanding comes from cultivating the nine functions of the prefrontal cortex: empathy, insight, response flexibility, emotion regulation, body regulation, morality, intuition, attuned communication, and fear modulation.[ii] The following are examples of some activities that help us cultivate these nine functions: self-growth workshops requiring self-reflection; good therapeutic relationships, such as with a licensed counselor; and healthy relationships with friends, family, and community. These activities cultivate interpersonal resonance, which occurs when attuned communication happens with another person. This type of stable, attuned connection in your relationships leads to empathy, insight, and better emotion and body regulation.

Let's take a moment to define some neuroscience terms that will be used throughout this book. The first is the prefrontal cortex mentioned in the last paragraph. This is the part of the brain inside the forehead area where higher reasoning comes from or "thinking about thinking." (See chart on the next page.) There are more furrows at your prefrontal cortex (that have more neurons) than any other part of the brain; scientists have likened this area to a super computer due to its virtually limitless capacities.

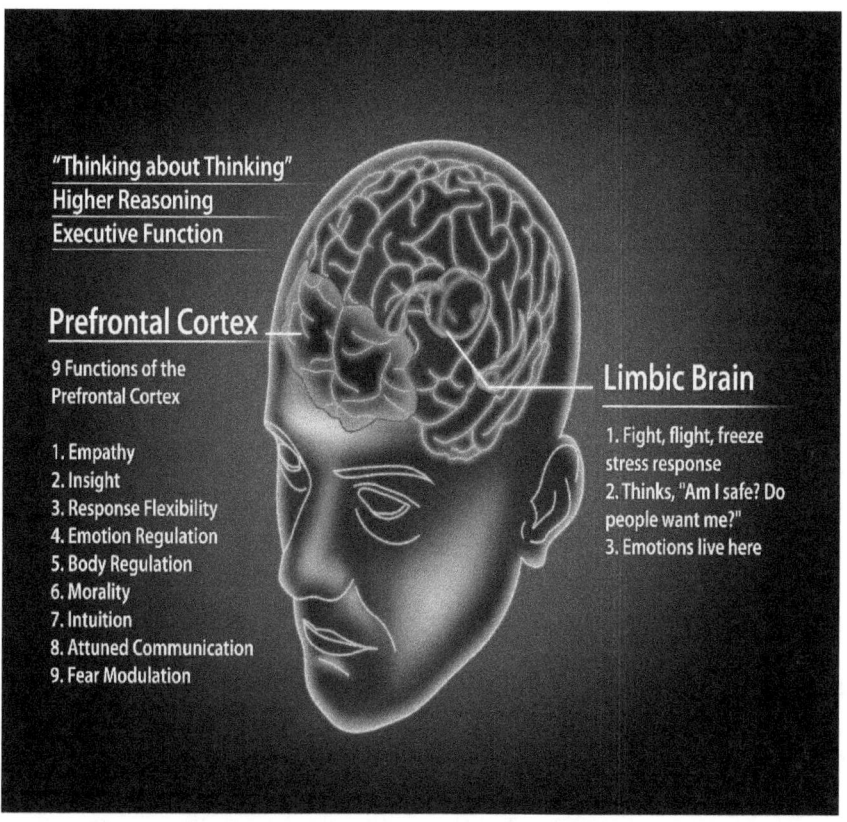

Your potential to find a life partner is similar to your prefrontal cortex: **your capacities are limitless to attract and maintain healthy relationships just as the capacity of the prefrontal cortex is limitless.** The book *Super Brain* and the following quote from Dr. Siegel touch on this limitless potential: "The mind uses the brain to create itself. As patterns of energy and information flow are passed among people within a culture and across generations, it is the mind that is shaping brain growth within our evolving human societies."

Beside this limitless potential, though, **we must take our knowledge and apply it in intelligent ways to achieve the outcome we desire.** This essentially is why I wrote this book: to help singles save time and emotional energy while finding a partner in an organized, logical way—not that dating or love is ever exactly logical.

Besides the prefrontal cortex, there is the limbic brain, (i.e., limbic system or limbic regions), which is located generally in the middle of the brain. From this area comes the fight, flight, and freeze stress response. When a person is in extreme fear, the prefrontal cortex is limited in its capacity to step in and use higher reasoning to bring about better choices because the limbic brain is firing away. In neurobiological terms, the competing functions of the limbic brain versus the prefrontal cortex coming together in a well-functioning whole is known as vertical integration (see chart on pages 29 and 30).[iii]

OK, so maybe you are wondering, "How are the nine functions of the prefrontal cortex and vertical integration related to a book on dating?" Firstly, a good dating outcome requires access to these nine functions of the prefrontal cortex; these functions improve when you cultivate vertical integration. You don't need to memorize the nine functions, just like you don't need to name the nine domains of integration. They are mentioned here as a framework to get us started talking about neuroscience and dating.

Dr. Dan Siegel, a UCLA researcher and psychiatrist, outlines nine domains of integration in his book, *Mindsight*. I represent these nine domains with the metaphor of the River of Brain Integration in this book. In neurobiology,

health (especially good emotional health) **is synonymous with integration**. The diagram on the next two pages shows different types of integration, but the idea here is that understanding and cultivating integration are key to improving your dating success and life happiness.

DOMAINS OF INTEGRATION

① Integration of Consciousness
Integrating the knowing and the known

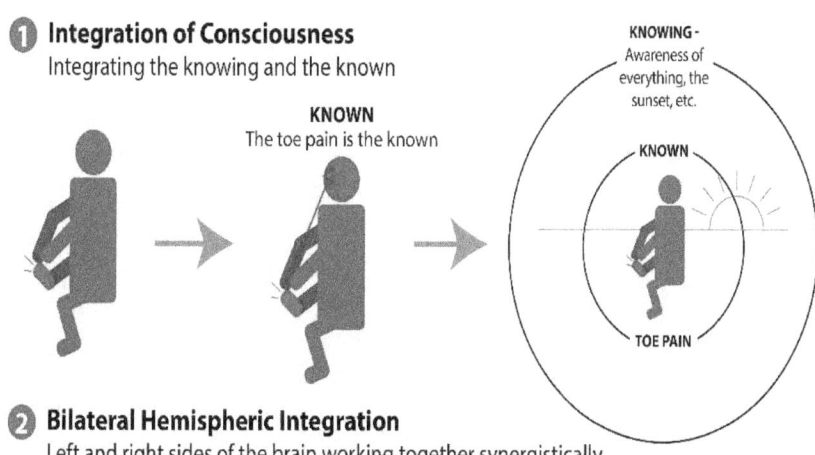

② Bilateral Hemispheric Integration
Left and right sides of the brain working together synergistically

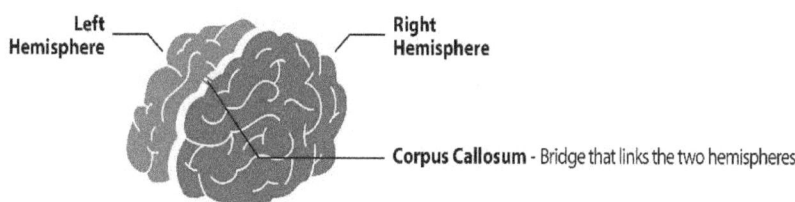

③ Vertical Integration
Head-to-toe nervous system integration

A. Prefrontal Cortex
B. Limbic Brain
C. Brainstem
D. Spinal Cord
E. Entire Nervous System

④ Memory Integration
Integrating explicit and implicit memory

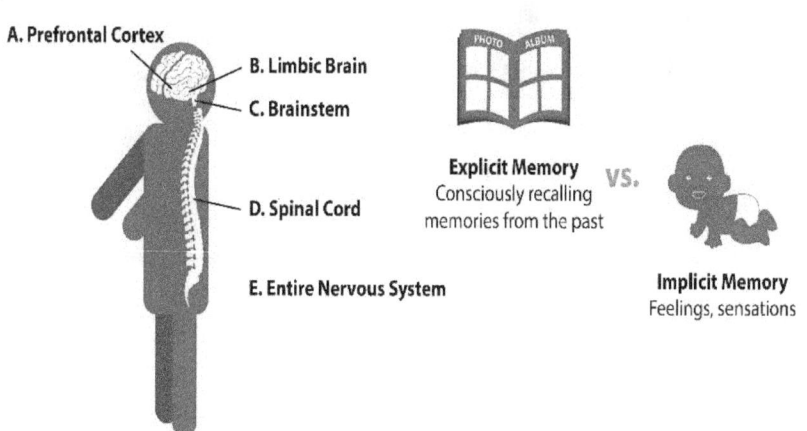

Explicit Memory vs. **Implicit Memory**
Consciously recalling memories from the past — Feelings, sensations

THE NEUROSCIENCE OF DATING

5. Narrative Integration
Using the skill of mental time travel (1.2.3.) to make sense of your life

IN PRESENT TIME
Jane thinking...

About her PAST and FUTURE

① ② ③

6. State Integration
Acknowledging different and sometimes competing states, learning to meet the needs of each state or mood instead of denial

HAPPY   SAD   ANGRY

A state can be a mood or different aspects of self such as serious worker or social butterfly

7. Interpersonal Integration
Connecting intimately in relationships while keeping our own identity

Happy Alone   Happy Together

8. Temporal Integration
Making sense of our mortality by integrating the competing functions of A and B

Ⓐ Ⓑ

Part of your brain that makes maps of time, past memories, future worries, this part knows you are mortal.

Part of your brain that seeks patterns and continuity (like when you blink you usually don't see the blink, you see one stream of vision).

9. Identity or Transpirational Integration
An expanded sense of self beyond "me" or "we" leading to a feeling of interconnectedness of all things. It is integrating all the above 8 domains of integration.

Cultivating integration involves bringing together different and competing functions of the body into a smoother, more coherent whole, especially in times of stress. And what is more stressful than dating?! All the decisions to make, the fear around safety, even becoming very excited (when your hopes are up), and the crashes with rejection and disappointment: these are examples of stress. How stressful is it just trying to figure out **where to begin** if you want to date online with so many websites?

Even with the most benign-seeming activities of dating, such as being on the computer looking at online profiles, intense emotions can be boiling underneath. And while some people detach from the emotions involved in the desire to meet a loving and stable partner, that doesn't mean the hopes and dreams aren't there.

From neuroscience research, Dr. Siegel writes, "When we block our awareness of feelings, they continue to affect us anyway. Research has shown repeatedly that even without conscious awareness, neural input from the internal world of body and emotion influences our reasoning and decision-making . . . in other words, you can run but you cannot hide."[iv] Achieving integration is about bringing awareness to all aspects of ourselves and making informed choices with that information, not denying parts of yourself.

Dating is certainly more stressful for some people

than others, but ultimately how you approach dating with your attitude and general plan can be a metaphor for how you approach life. Applying these teachings from neuroscience can be helpful not just in dating but also in life.

Finally, let's define "neurobiology" (which is the term that I use in this book to represent interpersonal neurobiology and relational neuroscience). Dr. Siegel defines it as, "a consilient field that embraces all branches of science as it seeks the common, universal findings across independent ways of knowing in order to expand our understanding of the mind and well-being…this field explores the ways in which relationships and the brain interact to shape our mental lives."[v] In another article he writes, "Interpersonal neurobiology is not a branch of neuroscience—it is not the same, for example, as social neuroscience. Instead, this field is an open forum for all ways of knowing to collaborate in deepening and expanding our way of understanding reality, the human mind, and well-being."[vi]

This book uses relational neuroscience as a map to optimize your process of dating. This book is not intended to be an explanation of neurobiology. Instead neuroscience terms are defined in a simple way and brought into the realm of dating.

SUMMARY

Interpersonal neurobiology (i.e., neurobiology) is a field of science that combines psychology, sociology, biology, and many different sciences to understand all ways of being and knowing the mind and what it means to be human.

There are two parts of the brain you should know: one is the prefrontal cortex, which involves higher reasoning, thinking about thinking, and uses skills like empathy, morality, and intuition. The other one is the limbic brain, where our stress response and emotions live. When these two parts of the brain work together synergistically, it is called "vertical integration."

Vertical integration is one domain of integration; neurobiology has nine, and the River of Brain Integration metaphor used throughout this book represents achieving all these different kinds of integration. To be our best self and to achieve Clarity, we should cultivate integration and the nine functions of the prefrontal cortex and screen others based on these criteria as well.

QUESTIONS

1. How clear do you feel about what you are looking for in a partner? Feel free to write a list (or complete the Target Exercise on page 127).

_____
_____
_____
_____
_____
_____

2. After making the list, use all your senses to feel, smell, taste, listen, and look into what it would be like to interact with someone with all these qualities and characteristics you seek from your list. It's important to believe love is out there for you; doing this exercise is a way to affirm (or cultivate) hope.

3. Which domains of the nine do you think are the most important in dating? Are you lacking in one particular domain? What could you do to improve it?

_____
_____
_____
_____
_____
_____

3 FASTLY FLOWING DOWN THE RIVER

It's September of 2010. I've moved to Athens, Georgia and started graduate school. I've been in a relationship mostly with one Dom since I created a profile on that darn kinky dating website, but there are red flags. One sign occurred about four months in, and we have already broken up then gotten back together again. Another breakup is looming. (It's not a good sign for the relationship if there are multiple breakups.)

I figured because I am closer to where said Dom lives, we would see each other more often. Wrong. Keep in mind we are texting throughout the day most days, and he doesn't live more than an hour away. I'm living in the area three weeks when I see him one afternoon. After that and an argument about rules, which he's furious with me for breaking but never actually explains, I break up with him. I'm also six weeks into graduate school, and luckily now I don't have as much time for bull sh*t.

Here's a tip if you're in an unhealthy relationship: join a program to learn something new. You'll meet new people and likely improve your self-esteem. In other words, find new activities that pull you away from the unhealthy relationship so that you have time and distance to reflect on whether what you are experiencing is what you want your life to look like.

Ask yourself, "If I write down what happens in the relationship on paper and other people read this, how are they going to react? How am I going to feel?" I myself feel embarrassed about the mistakes that I made with Dom, including giving away money (more on this in Protective Principles in Chapter 7.)

How available someone is can be a huge factor in dating. Some people will say they want a partner, **but their actions (and possibly body language) say, "I am too busy for you."** This is what confused me the most about Dom: he always said the right thing, but it wasn't translating into action. This balancing act between being flexible and adaptable in understanding a new partner while also feeling emotionally stable and secure with the budding relationship is both brain integration and successful dating in action.

FAST FLOW

Balanced integration requires equal amounts of flexibility, adaptability, and stability. These three terms are represented by the FAST flow down the River of Brain

Integration.[vii] The more Flexibility, Adaptability, and STability you cultivate, the FASTer you flow down the river, as opposed to ending up on the riverbanks of Rigidity and Chaos.

DRAW YOUR RIVER AND CLARITY BOAT BELOW:

River of Brain Integration

A metaphor for the nine domains of integration
which involve the nine functions of the prefrontal cortex

CHAOS

F.A.S.T

RIGIDITY

Flexibility
Adaptability
Stability

CLARITY
1. Defining Who You Are (boat)
2. Defining what you seek in a partner

In neurobiology, Flexibility means the ability to switch behavioral response according to the circumstances. Adaptability means being able to cope with adversity or danger without succumbing to basic emotions or impaired judgment. Stability means maintaining a consistent mood and emotional expression and being able not to become overly excited in serious situations. These metaphors of the FAST river flow and Rigidity and Chaos Riverbanks come from a tremendous amount of neuroscience research.[viii] Monitoring the quality of FAST flow for yourself and others can provide important clues in dating.

With said Dom, I was needing more STability. I certainly was not "maintaining a consistent mood and emotional expression." Looking back, I think we texted way too much instead of engaging in face-to-face activities that would have strengthened our prefrontal cortices and attuned communication.

When you have too much flexibility and adaptability, you end up on the riverbank of Chaos. This happened a lot for me when I was dating, as I tend to need more stability and have too much flexibility and adaptability. Your situation may be very different. If you have too much stability, you're on the Riverbank of Rigidity. Some people are so rigid and stable in their lives that they can't open their hearts and minds enough to find the love they are looking for and need.

QUESTIONS

1. What are you doing that limits your FAST flow down the river? Do you tend to be too stable or too flexible? _____
   _____
   _____
   _____
   _____
   _____

2. Since mindfulness meditation practice and securely-attached relationships strengthen the nine functions of your prefrontal cortex and enable a FASTer flow down the river, is there something new you are willing to try to improve your answer to #1? (See the next chapter for more data.) Two choices are having a five-minute daily meditation practice and seeing a therapist regularly.

_____

_____

_____

_____

_____

_____

4 YOUR 1-2-3 DATING TIPS

"Love is a fire. But whether it is going to warm your hearth or burn down your house, you can never tell."

—Joan Crawford

Optimal emotional health for the purposes of this book has been defined as FASTly flowing down the River of Brain Integration and avoiding the Riverbanks of Rigidity and Chaos.

Obvious Example of the Emotional Extremes in Dating, Not Integration

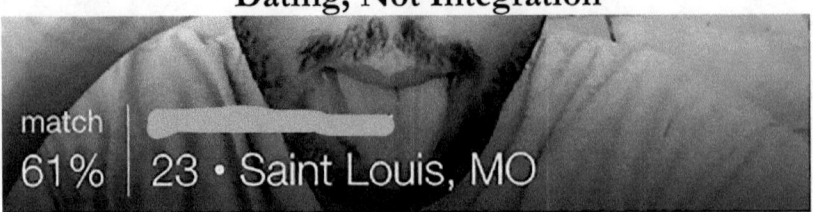

Oct 26

Damn girl!! You're gorgeous! how is a girl like you single? Are men just stupid?

Oct 29

Do you find me attractive?

Yesterday – 8:36pm

You are so F██████ UGLY!!!Why are you on this site, no man will ever want you...

As you reach out to connect with new, interesting singles who can spell, the skills needed in dating involve a combination of those nine functions of the prefrontal cortex, different domains of integration, and the **useful** aspects of Rigidity and Chaos.

Useful Aspects of Rigidity

Defended, discerning, skeptical, investigative, withholding, adulthood, believing in the brokenness of the world coming through in the actions of people, able to say no

vs.

Useful Aspects of Chaos

Undefended, curious, open, honest, innocence, vulnerable, believing in the underlying goodness of people, able to say yes

These qualities are in the chart on the next page. This principle in dating is explained further in Chapter 5. The important point here is that Good Rigidity Qualities are more important at the beginning of the dating process, and then Good Chaos Qualities are emphasized once the relationship has moved from casual dating to being more serious.

First Half	Second Half
Rigidity **Good Qualities**	**Chaos** **Good Qualities**
1. Discerning	1. Undefended
2. Investigative	2. Open
3. Adulthood	3. Innocence
4. Skeptical	4. Honest
5. Withholding	5. Curious
6. Believing in the brokenness of the world	6. Believing in the underlying goodness of people
7. Able to say No	7. Able to say Yes

#1 Online Profile Dos and Don'ts

One mistake that I see people make is putting too much or too little information on their online dating profile. When I point this out to the writer of the profile, people frequently get defensive, saying, "This is Who I Am. If someone doesn't like me for Who I Am, then I don't want to date them anyway." This response reflects a form of rigidity, which we don't want to be on the Riverbank of Rigidity.

My suggestion is that you put two or three interesting paragraphs about yourself, one or two sentences at most about what you are looking for, and always have a few good pictures including a profile picture and a full body picture. **Dating is all about cultivating a relationship and getting to know a person over time.** If you put all your eggs in one basket, wanting **every detail** about you to be on your profile or wanting to know **everything** about a person on the first date, you take some of the joy and mystery out of dating. You also are trending toward that Riverbank of Rigidity, and this tends to push people away. (Note: the author is available for consultation to review your profile and give suggestions at HeidiCrockett@gmail.com.)

What Not to Put on Your Profile (TMI)

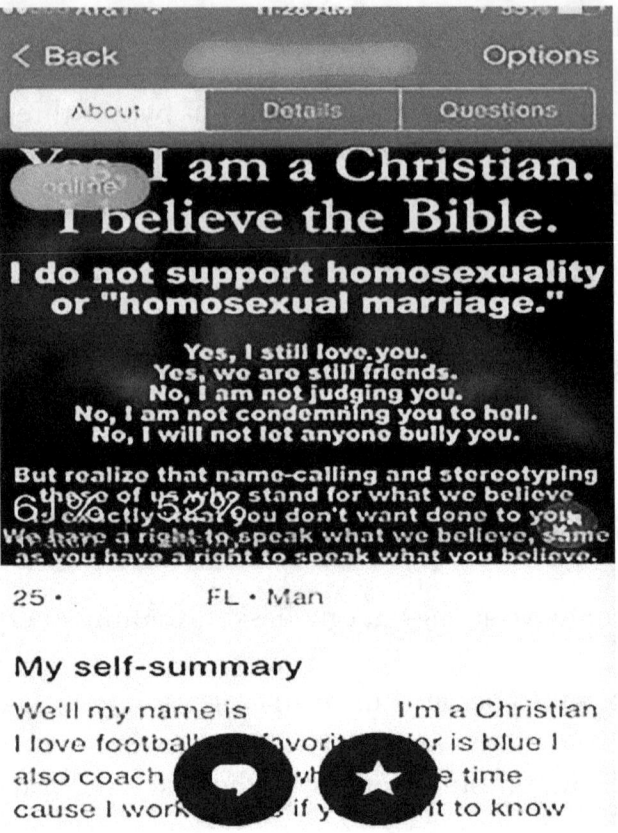

#2 Managing Your Time

Another big mistake that people make dating is a product of poor time management, especially in spending too much time on one potential match at a time. The following chart shows you the value of your time:

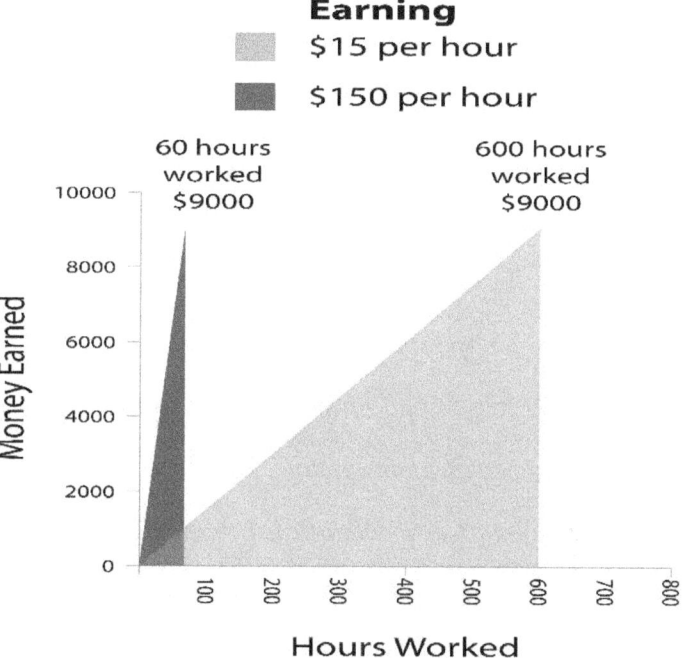
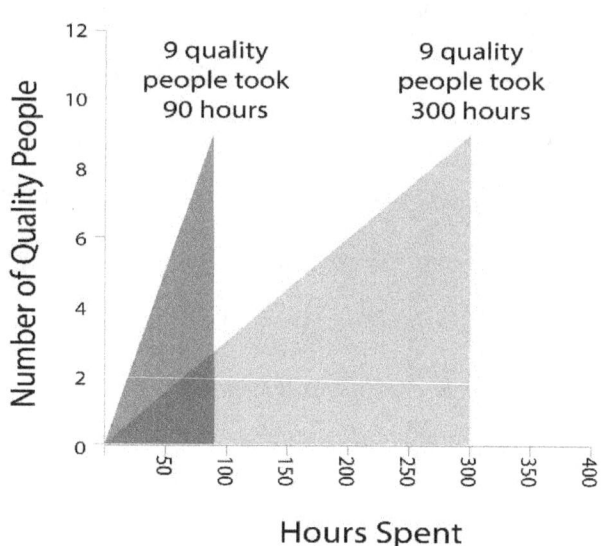

One single, Matt, talks about a recent date. (Note: Since he already had worked eighty-four hours that week, he wasn't having great time management in his professional life, much less with dating.)

> *I met a woman online locally. I wasn't really attracted to her but we had been chatting for 6 weeks or so and she was being persistent on meeting. I had been working 84 hours that week and I was exhausted. I really didn't feel like having company but she said we would watch Netflix and chill. I honestly didn't know the full meaning behind the whole Netflix and chill thing being recently divorced. She brought some beer and I don't really drink so after 2 I fell asleep. She rudely woke me up cussing me out telling me to take my clothes off and get in my bed!?!?!? She made me feel like I had to have sex with her. I started undressing and as I opened a condom she yelled at me that she wasn't a f****** whore! That was all I could take I had to ask her to get out…(back story) She had an agenda. She was wanting to get pregnant and knew my financial situation.*

When you are dating, you want to screen people

with agendas as much as possible as these people are **huge** time-wasters. Here's another dating story of someone with an agenda:

> *Met a girl on Plenty of Fish. We go to a nice restaurant. We are having good conversation and she asks where I live. I tell her where and mention that my landlord was planning on selling my house so I'd probably be moving in a few months. She starts grilling me on the square footage, location, condition of the house, asking price and then ends the date asking for my landlord's phone number. Never hear from her again.*

The Three-Step Time Check on the next page is one screening mechanism, and another one is time, as usually people reveal their true characteristics over time. (Since this unfolding of true character can take quite a bit of time, I suggest the Two Protective Principles in Chapter 7 to avoid making yourself overly vulnerable too soon.)

THREE-STEP TIME CHECK

 Your "first date" is by video chat (like Skype)

 Exchange a maximum number of six meaningful (detailed) messages before moving to a video chat "date"

 Limit your "first date" video chat to 15 minutes

THREE-STEP TIME CHECK

What I first recommend is using Skype or a video chat alternative when first meeting someone instead of doing an in-person date.[x] So, whatever Skype-like program you use, I recommend making your Skype username different from your real name and that the username be something real sounding like "Beth Stevens." (Erring on the side of safety, I also recommend that you not use your real name on your online profile. If your name is common like "John" or "Jennifer," then using your first name only is not as risky.) I also recommend that you only use your first name on the first two, in-person dates. It's better to be cautious in the beginning. Once you have your date's real name, look them up in your county for both civil and criminal cases. One woman I coached had been dating her seemingly perfect match for six weeks then found out that he was sexting other women on their date. She later found he had multiple legal complaints pending where he cheated customers and business partners. People often paint a good picture of themselves, and it's our duty to use our prefrontal cortex in the dating scene to check things out to protect our time, love, and energy. Never ignore your gut instincts.

Second, I recommend sending and receiving no more than six messages per potential match on the online dating platform before moving to the fifteen-minute Skype interview. This cuts down on time spent with people who are lying or fake. I know this advice might not work as well for heterosexual men as for single heterosexual women because the women will sometimes require more getting-to-know-you chatting time before being willing to move to a Skype-like meeting. Tweak this advice depending on your dating pool. For the technology challenged or those who prefer minimum technology, you might have to use your phone instead of Skype. Be sure to press *67 from a landline or "hide caller ID" on your cell phone before dialing the person's number to block your number for the first call.

Third, once you start talking with your date on Skype for the first time, tell them at the very beginning of the call that you have a meeting to go to and only have about fifteen minutes. This way if the person doesn't look anything like their profile pictures, their conversation is not coherent, or something else happens you don't like, you can be polite and get off in fifteen minutes, then send them a short e-mail telling them you are not interested. Remember the analogy that one certain key fits in one certain lock, so just because a key doesn't fit in your lock doesn't mean it's a bad key, it's just not the right fit.

This Three-Step Time Check guide ensures that the person does not have your real name or any contact information about you prior to the fifteen-minute Skype date and you have successfully pre-screened them. Good job! That is the first step in a longer process of getting to know someone. And when you actually get past those three steps with someone you like, you will feel like this:

When your date actually looks like his photo.

When It's Probably Better to Skip That First Video Chat Date…

When It's Probably Better to Skip That First Video Chat Date[xii]

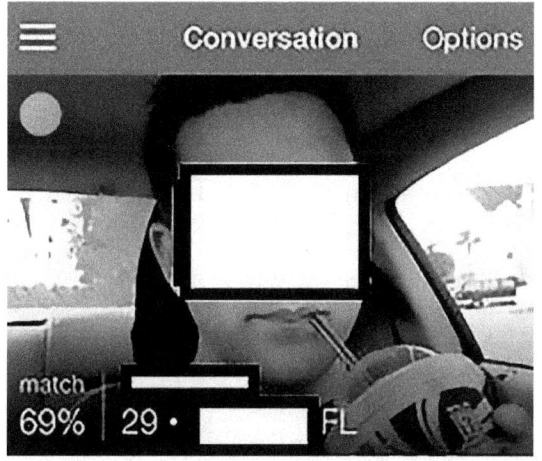

Some people have asked me, "What about people who don't have good communication skills on Skype or on the phone? Your three-step guide leaves these people out." I'll add that it is a matter of your personal judgment whether or not you want to move forward with trying an in-person date or another form of communication with the person. Some prefer texting to phone conversations, so that dating process might be different from the one suggested here. The issue with other online dating processes is that **you miss out on the opportunity to effectively screen a lot of time-wasters**. Your time is valuable! You want to meet the love of your life, but it doesn't need to take up an insane amount of your time and energy.

Messaging back and forth up to six times on online dating platforms allows you to see if the person is able to use coherent language, good grammar and spelling, and basic manners. You don't even need to suggest moving forward to the Skype chat if you see things that would rule out even using fifteen minutes of your time on Skype.

Using a dating app like Tinder (currently one of the

popular dating apps, but there are many) and choosing someone based on a picture and location could work **if you can move to a screening process**. A picture and location are quite basic information about someone that can easily go wrong. Here is one example:

> *I was on the Internet on a Saturday morning around 9 am and on some dating sites you can IM the person live if they are on. I get my first live IM ever and start talking to this girl. She is not at all bad looking. She asks what I was doing today, and I said nothing. She then asked if I wanted to hang out. She was only two miles away from where I lived and since I wasn't doing anything I said sure. I should have talked to her more or over the phone. Someone dropped her off in a large white van. It turns out she lived in a group home and suffered from severe head trauma from a car accident she had when she was 17 and the passenger died. She had seizures, and had to be watched, but was allowed to do normal things day to day, even meeting guys on dating sites.*

One thing that is so great about online dating is you

can screen people based on their education level, if they have children, or whatever specific criteria you desire. Of course, people lie so often on their profiles that that you do not want to spend too much time on any one person at the beginning. See more on lying in Chapters 6 and 7.

Another question that I'm asked is. "What if I want to spend more time getting to know the person online before we 'Skype' meet?" My suggestion is that you do the Skype meeting within the timeframe of exchanging six messages to confirm the person is more or less who they have told you that they are, then you can go back to getting to know e-mailing, if that works for you. (And remember that even a fifteen-minute Skype verify doesn't tell you about who that person is in their home and community environment.)

Many people have invested **insane** amounts of time only to discover huge lies about a person. Anyone who has watched the TV show *Catfish* knows this. Explain to your potential person that you very much want to respect their slower process for meeting/getting to know, but that you have been burned so many times that you need a visual/voice verification to continue the getting to know process. If the person is unwilling to offer you fifteen minutes of visual proof, that is suspicious. I always enjoyed when people would say they had an iPad first version with no camera or that they are a deaf mute and cannot talk to you. Do not waste your time with other people's games and time-wasting BS.

#3 Setting Limits Chart

SETTING LIMITS

Decide how many hours per week you want to invest in dating.

Categorize the total time into different parts of dating (and put the times on your calendar).

EXAMPLE FOR 3-HOUR WEEKLY PLAN

30 minutes on Tuesday night
Looking at new profiles, picking your favorites and sending messages to them

30 minutes on Thursday night
Reading received messages (paying more attention to the people that you picked and messaged) and replying including setting up video chat dates

2 hours on Saturday and Sunday
Connecting with new people either in-person, by phone, or via video chat

This last big mistake that I see online daters make is getting into one of those love/hate relationships indicative of those riverbanks of Rigidity/Chaos. You finally get the energy to create an online profile, then you check it every day, spending one or two hours each day, six days of the week. For heterosexual women, you spend too much time looking at people who write you instead of seeking out men that you are interested in and messaging them. Three weeks later, you are burned out on this online dating crap! Nothing works! In this example, the large amounts of time spent online dating for three weeks is like the Riverbank of Rigidity, where you rigidly online date (and during that rigidity you're not efficiently using your time either), checking messages and talking with people for large chunks of time, then you burn out and go into the Riverbank of Chaos, completely blowing off online dating and going out partying or doing other versions of giving up.

The neurobiological approach to dating involves flowing down that River of Brain Integration, meaning **you bring your search for love into alignment with other, equally important parts of your life.** "Setting Limits," the title of this section, means creating some guideline for yourself such as, "I will spend no more than three hours on my dating process each week." Maybe that involves one hour writing and reviewing profiles on Tuesday and Thursday then two hours on the weekend with Skype screening calls or in-person dates.

A further example of using neuroscience in dating means that you cultivate good relationships in your life and generally have fun with and outside of your established three-hours-per-week quest for a partner. If you tend to get heavily involved in a relationship after a few interactions, remind yourself that this is not indicative of brain integration and represents a form of Rigidity. Relationships are built over time, and partners are attracted to someone who has an enjoyable life with or without a significant other.

Love is mysterious and happens in an infinite

number of ways. I had my fifteen-minute Skype rule when I first met my current partner, Dr. Josh, online and Skyped with him for almost **three hours** the first time we talked. Obviously, what I am suggesting here are simple guidelines. The key is not that you will always be going by these guidelines, but that they can help save you so much **time and frustration**. Believe me!

Let me explain two examples of not flowing down the River of Brain Integration. Let's say that you frequently tend to get quickly involved in a relationship after a few in-person interactions, and dates tend to drop off interacting with you after about a month or two. Any time you see a pattern happening in your dating journey, it's important to cultivate those **nine functions of the prefrontal cortex and the nine domains of integration**. The same scrutiny is recommended if you repeatedly have great connections on dates, but you never move forward even though part of you wants a serious relationship. In both examples, there is a lack of integration between what you are consciously saying you want and what is happening. That lack of integration is worth exploring with a counselor or dating coach and a sign that it's time to strengthen those nine functions and nine domains.[xiii]

Nine Functions of the Prefrontal Cortex

Together these functions serve to connect the body proper, brainstem, limbic area, cortex, and input from other people. [i]

1. **Empathy**—The ability to see the world through another person's perspective [ii]

2. **Insight**—An inner sense of knowing [iii]

3. **Response flexibility**—The ability to respond flexibly... it allows the individual to pause and put a space between impulse and action. [iv]

4. **Emotion regulation**—Attaining enough intensity so that life has meaning, but not too much arousal for life to become chaotic or too little arousal for life to become rigid and depleted. [v]

5. **Body regulation**—Coordinating different systems of the body to function optimally...one example is balance between the sympathetic and parasympathetic branches of the autonomic nervous system.

6. **Morality**—The capacity to imagine, reason, and enact behaviors on behalf of a larger social good. [vi]

7. **Intuition**—A term that denotes the nonlogical knowing that emerges from the body, especially the neural networks in the heart and intestines that send their signals upward, through the insula, to regions of the middle prefrontal cortex. [vii]

8. **Attuned communication**—A compassionate connection in a relationship...one example is when internal states are the focus of attention and are "attuned to" such that they become "seen" by another person. [viii]

9. **Fear modulation**—The ability to unlearn a fear

If you've seen the pattern of dates dropping, cultivate **empathy** for your frustration at putting yourself out there and getting repeatedly rejected. Being dropped (see Ghosting section page 117) can mess up your brain integration and emotion regulation because of how it negatively affects your sense of a secure attachment to the world.

Cultivating empathy for yourself could mean taking a break from the heartache of rejection and trekking in Nepal with some friends. Try cultivating empathy for others with activities like volunteering to feed the homeless. Also, empathy doesn't have to equal action in the world; you can sit on a street corner and feel empathy for others; you can strengthen these nine functions by external action or the world of internal thoughts. Another important function is **insight**, which you can use to explore what you might be doing to lead to being repeatedly rejected. Of course, there is always the idea that you "just haven't met the right person," but patterns are great material with which to explore your self-understanding.

The same recommendation goes if you feel conflicted about a tendency not to move forward into a more serious relationship. You might cultivate **fear modulation**; if closeness is a fear then you can train you brain to unlearn it slowly. Or cultivate **response flexibility** if you tend to respond in the same way on dates. If you frequently go to sarcasm, try responding differently, such as with more empathy. It will feel awkward because it is a new pattern, but the point is to know that you are not fixed; you are changeable.

Exploring an example of this awkward feeling, Wendy Suzuki, a well-known PhD in brain research, decides to improve relationships in her life specifically with one doorman in her apartment in New York City. Right before going downstairs to speak with him, she describes "experiencing that sick feeling that comes before you take your most important final or right before you go on stage".[xiv] If changing your patterns seems too big to strangers on dates, start with your friends, coworkers, or acquaintances like how Dr. Suzuki practiced with her doorman.

Research demonstrates that all nine functions are the outcome of mindfulness meditation practice, and eight of the functions (all but intuition) are outcomes from secure attachment relationships.[xv] So beginning a meditation practice, even five minutes each day, and having connected conversations with close friends will help combat against stuck patterns and improve brain health.

Exercise is another important recommendation. Dr. Suzuki writes about all the brain benefits of meditation and exercise: "There is evidence that both activities provide clear brain benefits. Both provide striking mood enhancement . . . Both can increase the size of various brain structures, and both have positive effects on attention."[xvi]

Out of these three options—meditation practice, connected time with friends or family, and exercising—you might try the most uncommon for you—or better yet, try all three.

WHAT IF ONLINE DATING DOESN'T WORK FOR YOU?

Do you have Clarity that you won't use online dating, or is it coming from Rigidity? (See more about Clarity vs. Rigidity in Chapter 8.) As a dating coach, I think including some online platforms is an important part of an overall dating plan, but everyone is unique, and I've spoken with people who have good, understandable reasons for not online dating.

By only dating online you miss out on seeing people's in-person social skills as well as experiencing your own **intuition** with in-person contact. This is why I recommend moving to face-to-face video chat relatively quickly to make up for the information that gets lost by communicating in writing and pictures only.

However, by in-person dating only at random meetings or events, you miss out on the opportunity to screen your potential mate's level of education or other such factors that might be deal-breakers for you. (Of course, you can mediate this by going to events where your target person tends to attend.)

There are infinite ways of meeting singles. Check out Wayn.com or try traveling internationally with singles groups or staying in hostels. These are great ways to have fun and meet people. A basic Internet search will reveal speed dating events (unless you're over sixty; then they hardly exist) or other singles events like those found on Meetup.com. Figure out where your target audience (AKA, your dream partner) usually is, and go to those events.

Looking for single women around thirty? Try yoga classes or wine tasting events or dancing classes. Looking for single men around sixty? Try local singles, fishing, golfing, or travel groups aimed for 50+ crowd. My point is to understand your dating landscape.

Other options are EatWith.com, trying a new gym class, meeting singles at your faith community or a meditation group (where you're more likely to meet someone who shares your core values), and volunteering at an animal shelter or a charity that reflects your values. Other ideas are libraries, dog parks, and soup kitchens. For the eccentric single wear a stylish handmade bracelet on Etsy that lets people know you're single. There's a pin in the UK called "singlepin," but I don't think singles jewelry or clothing has taken off.

QUESTIONS

1. Do you tend to use the Good Rigidity Qualities more or the Good Chaos Qualities more when going on dates? Which qualities most resonate for you and why? _____
_____
_____
_____
_____

2. Name some examples where you are doing something different on your next date: _____
_____
_____
_____

3. Have you tried exercise, meditation, or a good connected friendship to help your brain in times of dating distress? Try increasing the frequency of all three of these to improve your overall health.

5 RIVERBANK OF CHAOS MISTAKES

One challenge in dating is people who want to be super honest and immediately put everything out on the table, which I call a Riverbank of Chaos mistake. An example can be found in this first text contact:

 3 minutes ago

 Hey beautiful. I'd love to get to know you if you are interested. I go to dialysis 3 days a week and need a transplant. I'm sweet and in college to be an RN. Want to text?

 No
✓ Read

 OK fatty

xvii

"Riverbank warning!" is usually my first response. If this is you, ask yourself, "What outcome am I seeking by revealing so much personal information about myself?"

Probably your behavior will not bring the outcome that you seek, so you might want to cultivate **response flexibility** and try new ways of relating and see if those new ways of relating help you obtain the outcome that you want.

"Too much too soon" could also be due to cultural differences or a lack of social skills. Regardless, be wary of too much sharing about yourself at the opening stages of dating. Next time, try asking the new date questions instead of talking about yourself so much.

If someone does this "too much too soon" to you, know that it is a sign of a lack of integration and that the person could have fewer of those nine functions of the prefrontal cortex skills. Remember **people are a product**

of their level of brain integration. In a way, their behaviors are not personal. Your date probably does this over-sharing to all people in their life. Some people have **personality disorders** (PD)--borderline PD, narcissistic PD, there are about a dozen PDs, which are enduring patterns of behavior. These people are essentially stuck in Rigidity, in Chaos, or alternating between both. Dr. Dan Siegel explains that "every brain imaging study of individuals with major psychiatric challenges reveals impaired integration in the brain." [xviii]

As a clinician, my advice is to try to recognize the level of brain integration that a person has in your initial interaction. If they are severely imbalanced, talk about shallower, less personal aspects like the weather or a favorite movie. If you observe attuned communication and empathy when relating, then move to sharing more personal information about yourself.

WRONG HALF

The skill of observing the level of your date's brain integration and acting accordingly can be summed up using the chart below.

First Half	Second Half
Rigidity **Good Qualities**	**Chaos** **Good Qualities**
1. Discerning	1. Undefended
2. Investigative	2. Open
3. Adulthood	3. Innocence
4. Skeptical	4. Honest
5. Withholding	5. Curious
6. Believing in the brokenness of the world	6. Believing in the underlying goodness of people
7. Able to say No	7. Able to say Yes

I call over-sharing the Wrong Half, using the analogy of soccer games and their two halves. The mistake is having a second-half-of-the-game mindset at the very beginning instead of approaching it from a first-half point of view.

Anyone who has done this a few or a few dozen times understands some of the pitfalls; there is disproportionate revealing of personal information on one side that leaves the person who over-shared feeling vulnerable.

When you or your date are not flowing down that River of Brain Integration, Wrong Half behavior tends to happen. Revealing too much personal information too soon can leave you feeling overly vulnerable, while the receiving side possibly quits "the game" abnormally fast. Thus, leaving the revealer stranded on a riverbank, bewildered and confused.

When it's a quick "game over," we might use our prefrontal cortex and ask ourselves, "What happened?!" Somewhere along the way attuned communication and shared empathy stopped happening, or maybe the person didn't care about you, didn't get what they wanted, and left. In either case, though, it can be useful to investigate and understand what happened and why.

Two important things could be happening when there is a Wrong Half. The first is that you could be burned out on dating, lonely, and using the dating process as a substitute for necessary friendships and meaningful relationships. If this is true, then there are things you can do (like spending more time with friends and taking a break from dating) and some behaviors that you will want to modify when you are in the first half of dating (like being aware of how your feelings of loneliness might be negatively affecting your dating process early on and instead lovingly back-burner the loneliness and focus on the other person or the future). The overall dating technique that I am suggesting here is that the **river flow should start out shallow and move to deeper waters over time.**

The second thing that could be happening in dating

is a replaying of dysfunctional patterns you learned in childhood. Whenever we over-reveal (or under-reveal) personal information in the process of cultivating relationships, this is an opportunity to reflect on the patterns of relating we developed when young. We can ask ourselves, "Was that relating behavior from childhood healthy, or did I develop that behavior as a coping mechanism?" and, "Does that relating behavior produce good results for me today?"

Brain integration and good mental health are about cultivating the ability to be open to change and try new things. We don't have to think of ourselves as any one, fixed way. One tenant of good brain health is to do things differently, such as drive to work using a new route, brushing your teeth with your opposite hand, or using a different toy from usual to spank your partner.

You can stretch your brain's capacity in relating to

others too, such as by going to a social event and not being your usual self for an evening. You could go to an event you would not normally attend and practice being more outgoing (or quieter). If it helps, you could wear something physical like a bracelet or a hat that reminds you that you are trying on a different personality for a day. Cultivating this willingness to change and try new things will help develop integration and creativity.

Let's say you are wondering whether what happened was a Wrong Half or that you weren't a match, and you tell yourself the cheesy (but useful) affirmation: **There's no such thing as rejection, only selection**. Some people think, "Maybe I screened out this person by revealing so much personal information and they didn't like me?" This is a tough question to answer, especially if a date suddenly disappears. My biggest recommendation is to **ask**. Of course, this isn't possible if you are ghosted.

Dating is an ongoing learning process, and if patterns start happening for you, your best bet is to get information outside of yourself to see how others are experiencing you. This is why a dating coach can be helpful, and getting information straight from the source can be invaluable, as long as you think that source is worth asking.

If you find out that revealing that terrible story that happened during your childhood on the second date rubbed the person the wrong way, ask them what was most uncomfortable about hearing the story. If your date says they just don't want to hear all those messy details early on in dating, maybe ask if they are willing to go on another date and talk about career goals or life dreams. In other words, continue to connect with the person and be curious if genuine interest remains underneath. Relationship building is about cultivating curiosity and empathy.

Unfortunately, whenever there is a Wrong Half, the likely response is cutting off the relationship. **As far as cultivating good emotional health, a cutoff is unhealthy for your brain.** A cutoff without explanation isn't helpful and can cause pain, especially from the feeling of rejection. In an online forum for bad dating stories, one person writes:

> *After a year and a half he ghosted me and I am physically and mentally in pain. I can't eat or sleep. I'm lost, confused, and miserable. I have sent him countless messages but for nothing. This is hell someone please help me understand so I can move on!*

The dating world, capitalism, and Tinder all speak to this disposable, always-more-to-buy or more-people-to-date mentality. Like this text message exchange:

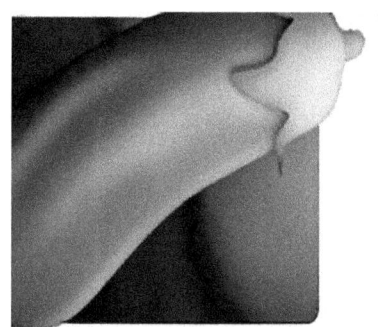

 Ok

It's not really a way to approach me, probably messaging and getting to know me would've been a better idea

I don't know you

I don't send nude photos to people I don't know. sorry

Who cares your not that important

Write a message...

 There's more woman to find

xix

When I speak about the brokenness of the world in this book, I am referring to this mentality. Experiencing more cutoffs and false representations of what is truly real and good creates an unhealthy detachment (brokenness) that replicates itself in actions to others (broken world). It's kind of like how consuming a manmade chemical like the artificial sweetener aspartame (which the body doesn't recognize because it doesn't occur in nature) creates free radicals in the body. These free radicals lead to bad health outcomes. In other words, consuming cutoffs leads to the free radicals of cutting off other people, which just makes the world uglier and less fun for everyone.

One small example of this false representation of goodness is Febreze's motto "Breathe happy." What about breathing a product full of chemicals known to cause cancer makes someone happy? Smelling it causes asthma symptoms in me.[xx]

If you are looking for a loving, long-term partner, your relationships must be valuable. (In other words, you have to be willing to repair the brokenness of the world by doing your best not to replicate it when possible.) Not everyone is going to be interesting or someone you want to spend time with, but you can have the value to treat people with kindness, even if your lock and their key don't fit. As Hermes Trismegistus said, "As above, so below, as within, so without, as the universe, so the soul."

Dating involves a combination of the useful aspects of Rigidity and Chaos. Dating is both a cold-hearted, time-consuming process of screening people (essentially treating them like objects) and an incredibly meaningful opportunity to represent who you are and what your values are. How you treat each person that you interact with is a reflection of your values.

Meanwhile, let's face it, it can get **exhausting** to seek for the support and love from another person and to receive drama and pain instead. It can get exhausting to be respectful and kind to each person you meet, especially if you are working full-time with emotionally or physically draining clients or if you are already caring for children and/or parents. This is why I recommend setting limits and time management to place the appropriate value on different aspects of your life and apply that value to how you invest your time.

QUESTIONS

1. Do you tend to under-share or over-share when you are on your first or second date?_____

2. If you did the opposite of what you normally do, name some things that you might say or do on your next date: _____
_____
_____
_____

3. Think of someone that does not have a high level of brain integration. What does that person do or say to let you know this?_____
_____
_____

4. Taking into account that a person with a low level of integration is often permanently stuck in Rigidity or Chaos or both, what can you tell yourself or do to make future interactions easier? (Remember the suggestion to talk about more shallow, less personal

subjects.) _____

_____

_____

5. Name some examples of how the brokenness of the world has affected you: _____

_____

_____

_____

6. Do you agree or disagree that your actions to not replicate the brokenness of the world make a difference? If agree, write some examples of actions you plan to take in the future. If disagree, articulate why:_____

_____

_____

_____

7. What can you do to express the value of your closest relationships? And to cultivate future valuable relationships?_____

_____

_____

_____

6 DISHONESTY FROM WITHIN

"I do not trust people who don't love themselves and yet tell me, 'I love you.' There is an African saying which is: Be careful when a naked person offers you a shirt."

—Maya Angelou

Not everyone is going to agree with the concepts around honesty and dating discussed in this chapter. I encourage the reader to keep an open mind. The basic advice here is to have integrity (that matters the most), but a small amount of lying, such as on your online dating profile, is OK and possibly recommended in the First Half of dating. I just wish there were another word besides "lying" because it sounds really bad.

In social work, there's a term, therapeutic fibbing, which is "a controversial yet very effective method of dealing with the anxiety experienced by many people with Alzheimer's and other dementias. In essence, it is telling a 'fib' in order to avoid increased anxiety and agitation in a person with dementia."[xxi] I too have found it to be a "very effective method" in my experience as a geriatric social worker with dementia cases and in dating. Small lies are effective in that they can help you achieve your goal of getting face-to-face with potential matches. For example, I wouldn't have met my current partner if he hadn't lied about his age on his online profile. (He may kick me in the butt for writing that in this book, but hey, I'm trying to be **honest** about dishonesty, and what a perfect example!)

Most of us have lied at some point in our lives. I even suggested it in my Three-Step Time Check protocol when you tell your Skype date that you only have fifteen minutes before you have to go to a meeting. Most people lie a little bit (or a lot) when online dating. (I don't agree with the "lying a lot" approach as the more a person lies, the more it shatters their integrity and character which is one thing that you are screening for with online dating.)

Here is one obvious example of recommended lying: if someone is forty, if they are comfortable with it, I say put "39" on their online dating profile. The reason is that good people will screen you out because of a number. Being born six months before your current birthday could mean the difference between having the chance to meet your correct match and their pre-screening you out forever. There is a balance between honesty and understanding the dating game. Let's jokingly call this the tenth domain of integration: Dating Game Integration.

Examples of ambiguous scenarios with lying would include a cancer survivor who wonders if they should put that on their online profile. Some might say it is lying by omission. What if someone is looking for a lover but is married and their spouse is in a memory care facility with end-stage dementia? Some might say this caregiver who's been caregiving for fifteen years is breaking their marriage vows, whereas others may feel the person is not truly married anymore because the person has advanced dementia. Everything is open to interpretation. What matters is that whomever you date is eventually going to have to understand your **narrative integration**: how you make sense of your life story and life circumstances including why you chose to lie in your initial contact with the person and on your online profile.

I suggest that **within two in-person dates that any lie from your online profile be confessed** and you understand that it may cause an already burned person to drop you forever. (That person's 100% dropping you is a form of Rigidity since dating is a getting-to-know process, especially if you can explain your reasons for the lie.) Being dropped is the risk you take because dating is all about weighing the risks and benefits about literally everything. Other more personal information like being a cancer survivor is a yellow zone of uncertainty. Some dating advice books recommend telling on the fourth date, but you really have to decide what is right for you.

You can also adapt to the dating environment by expecting some level of lying. One example of adapting is how I started asking first dates, "So what's your real age?" because I learned that almost everyone lies about that.

SELF-DECEPTION

How might you be lying to yourself in big or small ways? The truer you are to Who You Are including your values and life priorities and the more you live these out in your life (walk your talk) the more attractive you will be to a potential partner and **the more likely you will be to attract the right match for you.**

An interesting finding from neuroscience is that as you grow in self-understanding and cultivate those nine functions and nine domains, you are more likely to experience a feeling of connectedness with others and a feeling of altruism and wanting to give back. This connectedness is an outcome of the ninth domain of integration known as identity integration or transpirational integration in neurobiology. This is the final domain of integration, where you are integrating integration. The less we engage in self-deception, the more we are able to come together in a coherent whole and achieve higher levels of integration, including identity integration.

SUMMARY

Lying a little bit on your online profile is not the end of the world, but if you lie a lot, you are a douchebag. Because we are covering the subject of whether or not you lie, reflect on ways that you might lie to yourself and try not to do that. Lying to yourself is the opposite of brain integration and creates a schizoid dichotomy that likely leads to confusion and drama. The goal in integration is to be clear and undivided inside, not to be so undecided that one part of you does one thing (like overeating), but another part of you wants something different (like losing weight). In this sense, wherever there is not integration, that is worth exploring, perhaps with a counselor or coach or a self-growth workshop. Places like the Omega Institute, Rowe Conference Center, Kirpalu, and many more have catalogs with amazing workshops to choose just what you need. Also, come to Hippocrates Health Institute to hear the author present on relational neuroscience in-person and the Psychotherapy Networker is a fascinating, conference every March with self-growth tips for busy professionals.

QUESTIONS

1. Are you OK with the idea of therapeutic fibbing for online dating? If OK, what might you change about your online profile or in making initial contact with someone? If not OK, write why:___

   _____
   _____
   _____
   _____
   _____

2. Is there an area of your life that lacks integration (where one part of you wants one thing and another part of you wants something else)? What could you do to improve? _____

   _____
   _____
   _____
   _____

7 DISHONESTY FROM OTHERS

"I have to go. I have a finite amount of life, and I don't want to spend it arguing with you."—Jenny Trout

During my dating fails, I learned two important principles to minimize the heartache that comes from others' dishonesty. I realized that as long as I applied the following Two Protective Principles that dating hiccups were able to fall mostly like water off a duck's back (like when someone lied to me about being married and my discovering it on a second date).

The advice in this chapter is vital because others' dishonesty can quickly cause a genuine person to crash their boat into the Riverbanks of Rigidity or Chaos. (In this case, such a crash would be directly a result of spending time with someone who is likely already stuck on a riverbank.) These crashes mean our flowing dating journey comes to a sudden halt whenever we encounter painful life situations created by less-than-ideal people. Our goal in dating is to get better at prescreening people before in-person dates to avoid these riverbank crashes altogether and to learn ways to get back in the FAST flow as quickly as possible with minimal emotional drain.

TWO PROTECTIVE PRINCIPLES

1. Don't make yourself financially vulnerable.
2. Don't make yourself sexually vulnerable.

These two principles will protect you from the long-term side effects of dating as long as you define what it means **for you** to be financially and sexually vulnerable.

Remember in Chapter 2 when I broke up with my Dom and admitted to giving him money? (As in thousands of dollars, like "idiot" tattooed to my forehead.) While it is embarrassing to admit, that was not the last time that I loaned money to a boyfriend!

Come on, I had to mess up one more time.

Why did I loan money to people when I **knew** it was a bad idea?! Even my intuition told me better.

I remember the nagging feeling clearly while I was writing the check, but I did it **anyway**. My dumb behavior always came after I had made myself sexually vulnerable. We do **stupid things** when we have dopamine and oxytocin like crack-cocaine pulsing through us. This is why I have a PowerPoint slide entitled, "**Warning**: Stupid in Love," from my presentations on dating fun and safety. My PowerPoint slide has two quotes from Dr. Stella Resnick:

"A person in love may have
impaired decision-making ability."

and

"The lack of blood flow to these areas
suggests reduced function in judgment,
decision making, and the assessment of social situations."[xxii]

It's worth pointing out that the trigger for my stupidly loaning money was always being presented with the person that I cared about, who was in tremendous distress and need; either they had sheer panic about the IRS or they were looking for housing and needed help with a deposit. Because of my empathy, I felt their pain and wanted to make it better. I didn't use logical thinking that these people had the same amount of money that I had and realize that they just had different spending priorities. Instead, I felt extremely sorry for them and gave them money that I now regret. In those moments, my empathy took a twisted dark path, and I crashed onto the Riverbanks of Compassion and Others. (See Chapter 8 for more on these Riverbanks.)

Oftentimes we don't know that we've been made financially or sexually vulnerable until **after** our mistakes, when we've had time to reflect on what went wrong. This is how we use our prefrontal cortex in dating. We think about the past and future and make new decisions about what actions we want to take going forward.

I found that while past boyfriends of mine had red flags from the very beginning, they pushed me around because I'd become sexually vulnerable and emotionally invested. Over time, I had to train myself to see the red flags sooner and set up guidelines to prevent vulnerability, so that I could politely separate myself from the person and continue on my journey to find the correct match.

SEXUAL VULNERABILITY

I decided to define certain sex acts as making me sexually vulnerable, and I needed those acts not to be included in dating. Thus, I didn't want to make myself that sexually vulnerable and engage in those certain sex acts until the relationship became serious. Also, after I learned that sexual arousal leads to impaired decision-making (from the above quotes), as does alcohol and other drugs, I gained greater Clarity about why it was important to stay away from those sex acts that made my prefrontal cortex all mushy with poor judgment. (As a side note, **many** of the worst-ever dating stories I've heard involved alcohol or drugs.)

See the questions at the end of this chapter and contemplate, "What makes me sexually vulnerable?" as well as "What actions do I need to take that reflect my definition and to protect me?"

FINANCIAL VULNERABILITY

Do you remember Matt's story in Chapter 3? He saw that a date had an agenda to get pregnant because of his financial status. In his case, being financially vulnerable included unprotected sex. In his plan, protecting himself from sexual and financial vulnerability would include using condoms.

I think it's important to say that men might define vulnerability differently from women, but defining both financial and sexual vulnerability is important for both genders. I know men who carry low-grade resentment about the financial burden of playing the dating game and who cannot afford expensive dinners. Some of these men went through periods where they did not date because they were broke and embarrassed about it. These feelings of shame and guilt coming from within us and from society must be looked at more closely. I created the two

Protective Principles after I better understood the guilt and shame that I went through in my dating process. **If you can define what sexual and financial vulnerability mean to you and set boundaries, you'll avoid what could be some very costly mistakes.**

GENERAL SAFETY

Do con men and women know these Two Protective Principles? They certainly do because they specialize in observing people's vulnerabilities and know how to recognize people whom they can easily con. This is why the highest number of scams are aimed at seniors, the most vulnerable large population with money.

If you are meeting someone for the first time, consider having a plan where you notify a friend before and after the date. Text a friend where you are going and the name of the person you are meeting along with their phone number. Establish an approximate timeframe for when you will tell your friend that you are safe and the date is over. You can even have a safe word like "chicken" and establish that if you text or say the word on the phone, it means you are not safe and the person should call the police. (Just don't forget your word and use it accidentally!)

All the skills outlined in this book are to protect you against con artists and to save you time and heartache. If you can set limits on your time when screening people, if you can have rules and phrases ready for when you go "stupid in love," you'll be better protected. (Examples include, "I always use barriers with new partners," and, "I have a rule that I will not loan money to friends because it's caused me to lose friendships in my past.") Repeat whatever phrases that you want to use and have them more strongly imbedded in your neural network. Focus on the areas where you are weakest and come up with a plan to protect yourself.

SEX AND SAFETY

"Silence is the greatest risk of sexual health."
—Dr. Leslie Schover

Being a Certified Sexuality Educator with AASECT, I feel that it's important to add some advice about dishonesty and sex. Some people will lie (silence) about whether or not they have sexually transmitted infections (STIs). Knowing this, it is important to:

1. Establish guidelines to protect yourself.
2. Relax about things that are out of your control.

This middle-ground approach with both #1 and #2 applies whether you are screening people to go on first dates or discussing sexual health. Likewise, the advice to set limits (on page 64) matches the advice in this section to think through and decide ahead of time what is right sexually for you. Thus, we are using our prefrontal cortex to think about thinking and being a conscious adult about our sex choices as we steer our boat down the River of Sex Integration.

They are **many** fun, intimate acts that do not put a person at risk. Why does sex have to look any one way? It is up to you to decide what expressions of love and pleasure look like. For more information about activities that minimize risk, see Appendix 3: Sex Risk Spectrum.

An easy guideline with choosing to be sexually active is having a Panel Party if you plan to have unprotected sex. A Panel Party is simply both people getting a full STI panel and exchanging those results with each other (as in **physically looking at the paper STI reports**, not verbally exchanging what those reports hypothetically said).

Remember that new HIV antibodies can take up to six months to show up, so you would not be 100% sure about your partner's HIV status unless you exchanged STI panels and then did a second exchange six months later.[xxiii] (Make sure you ask your doctor to include all STI tests; sometimes they leave certain ones out unless you are clear. **It's best to go in with a list ready of the STI tests that you want to be included in the panel.**)

Even more important to point out, though, is the fact that **at any point in time your partner could be engaging in (unprotected) sexual activity that they are not disclosing to you.** Thus, your partner could be causing you **risks that you don't even know about**. Similarly, your partner might not even know that they have an STI (which is another reason to do the Panel Party as you could be helping someone else out, too). I know that discussing sex and dishonesty is the **antithesis** of what you are seeking in finding a life partner. Nevertheless, we must look at the reality of the dating scene, the appropriate place of trust, and then making informed, intelligent choices.

Hey, you could even have it written in your **marriage vows** that you both do a panel party once a year and share the results.

Do people actually do the Panel Party? The answer is both yes and no. The question is how much you trust the person that you are talking with about these things. Having witnessed the frequency with which people lie in dating (and in marriage) I would say that it's a pretty logical conclusion to err on the side of doubt. Note that I did not write "err on the side of paranoia"; I wrote "doubt," meaning have a healthy level of skepticism and possibly some guidelines to protect yourself and your lover.

Even if you use a condom or a female condom it doesn't protect you against the human papilloma virus,

HPV. The only way to protect yourself is to discuss your number of sex partners within the last year or so if you plan to be sexually active with someone and limit numbers, as higher numbers put you at greater risk for acquiring different HPV strains. In 90% of cases, HPV resolves itself within two years, although you can get genital warts from certain strains.[xxiv] The main fear with HPV is its link to cervical cancer. (Side note: please read *Vaccines 2.0: The Careful Parent's Guide to Making Safe Vaccination Choices for Your Family*, by Mark Blaxill and Dan Olmsted, if you have questions about the HPV vaccine.)

Just think about the **risk to your health**: having unprotected sex and acquiring (worst case scenario) HIV could shorten your life and significantly impact the rest of your life. You have to ask yourself (before you are in the heat of the moment and your judgment and decision-making capacities are impaired): "Do I care about myself enough that I will protect my health? Will I jeopardize my entire future for one night of hot sex?"

In addition to being aware of STI risks, **an important factor in sexuality education is your self-esteem**. Low self-esteem makes you more vulnerable and less likely to speak up and protect yourself. For more information see Appendix 1: Self-Esteem Resources. Having securely attached relationships whether with friends or as modeled by a counselor can significantly improve self-esteem. Learning how not to make yourself sexually or financially vulnerable applies to **all adults**, whatever your life circumstances. **Defining those two things and sticking to what you decide will make you a much happier, healthier person.**

At the same time, who wants to go around thinking that everyone is out to get them? In the eyes of the general population, you might be seen as overly paranoid by say, asking for a Panel Party. **Better to be accused of being paranoid than sick or dead! Pay attention to how susceptible you are to other people's criticism, and cultivate strengthening your own inner sense of knowing.** This will make you a more successful, happier person and will help you to attract a good life partner. Susceptibility to criticism can be seen as falling onto the Riverbank of Chaos, and strengthening your own inner knowing can be better explained as cultivating equal amounts of FAST (Flexibility, Adaptability, and STability) to FASTly flow down your River of Brain Integration.

Likewise, succumbing to the pressure to be different from Who You Are could be seen as Chaos, and staying exactly how you are and not doing anything suggested in this book (then complaining online dating doesn't work for you) could be seen as excessive Rigidity. You must define your own versions of Rigidity and Chaos. Only you know the answers.

Besides knowing about STI risks, it's important to pay attention to the **fear** associated with sexual activity and the lack of talk about **pleasure. Flowing down your River of Integration can (and should) be pleasurable.** The intoxicating fresh air of nature, the exhilaration of floating on our boat, even soaking in the kind touch or gaze of concern from a friend: these are all forms of pleasure. Fear can be exciting in sex play when it is used right, meaning the partners have established trust and safety beforehand; **excessive** fear and anxiety in a relationship are usually red flags that you have crashed onto a Riverbank of Rigidity or Chaos. Cultivating those nine domains will help you put all your different feelings, including fear and pleasure, in their proper place in your boat.

GHOSTING AND WHAT TO DO ABOUT IT

For those who don't know, "ghosting" is a dating term meaning someone that you thought cared about you suddenly disappears forever with no explanation. One blog post writer describes ghosting:

> *It still felt a bit like someone had punched me in the gut when it happened. The disregard is insulting. The lack of closure is maddening. You move on, but not before your <u>self-esteem</u> takes a hit. The only thing worse than being broken up with is realizing that someone didn't even consider you worth breaking up with.*[xxv]

Another ghosted person's story:

> *Dated a girl for almost two years and breaks up with me via Facebook message. She wanted to avoid confrontation and would offer no explanation as I thought things were going well. Would refuse to meet up, call back, or even text back.*

Trying to offer a short paragraph about what to do about ghosting is similar to the advice that I gave about

Clarity in Chapter 1. It is something deeply personal, and you have to make a decision on your own as to its meaning in your dating journey.

I can point out some likely responses in your brain.

Ghosting can cause you to crash quickly on those Riverbanks of Rigidity or Chaos, depending on which riverbank you favor when under stress. If you tend to be stable in your life and need more flexibility and you get ghosted, probably your response will be becoming extra rigid with dating. Maybe you **stop dating completely** for a certain period of time. If you tend to be very flexible in your life and need more stability, ghosting could result in your crashing into the Riverbank of Chaos. Maybe you **start dating a lot** of new people to compensate. Remember, we need equal amounts of Flexibility, Adaptability, and STability to flow FASTly down the River of Brain Integration.

The same neurobiological principles in this book apply to even those most difficult dating moments, including being ghosted. Use the nine functions of your prefrontal cortex to think about thinking and reflect on your experience. Cultivate **attuned communication** with a counselor or good friend to feel cared about in the face of that ghosting rejection, and stabilize your sense of self-worth (and strengthen that earned-secure attachment style). Have **empathy** for yourself, for your efforts and frustrations on your dating journey. Use a dating coach to help you re-focus on your dating goals, perhaps after taking a time-out to recover from the pain of ghosting. Have empathy not only for yourself but also for everyone who has ever been ghosted, and recommit to your values on how you communicate to others in dating.

WHAT IF I WANT TO GHOST SOMEONE?

There are ways that you can say no to people while honoring your integrity and treating others with the kindness and respect that you want for yourself. It can be as simple as a "No, thank you." If you do the fifteen-minute Skype session and for obvious reasons the date is not a fit, you can send a short e-mail saying that it is not a right fit for you.

Some people don't do well with rejection and will get upset no matter how well you try to frame your no. Just remember the behaviors that match your integrity, and if you need to cut-off from a person, then do it and do it without guilt.

QUESTIONS

1. How do you define what it is for you to be made financially vulnerable? What amount of money (budget) is OK to spend on dating and when? Make

a list of fun activities that you could do on a date that will not go over your budget._____

_____
_____
_____
_____
_____

2. How do you define what it is for you to be made sexually vulnerable? What amount of intimacy (sex) is OK when dating and when? Make a list of activities that you consider within your comfort zone and when they are OK for you. What can you do now to help remind yourself of your decision here when you are experiencing the effects of being stupid in love in the future (when you have hormones rushing through your system and your judgment is impaired in the moment)?_____

_____
_____
_____
_____
_____

3. Think about a time when you were more vulnerable than usual and someone took advantage of that. What have you done since then to protect yourself? Does what you are doing to protect yourself bring you peace of mind, or do you find that it causes you more fear and anxiety? (Sometime we get stuck in patterns and behaviors that aren't producing the results we seek.)_____

    _____

    _____

4. Consider visiting some evidence-based websites on STIs (see links in the Appendix and on my website: RedLightHeidi.com). How informed do you feel about STI risks? Is there anything you could do to better protect yourself? Being prepared with protection and pre-established phrases can help. Try, for example, "Your condoms or mine?" or, "I have this fun new sampler kit; which do you want to try?"_____

    _____

    _____

    _____

    _____

8 RIVERBANK OF RIGIDITY MISTAKES

I partially blame the storybook line, "And they lived happily ever after," and the common portrayal of love and sex in movies for our crap dating scene. We have millions of singles walking around with brains full of ridiculous expectations having nothing to do with real life. These expectations crash against each other in dramatic explosions date after date and relationship cut-off after relationship cut-off. It's like the **opposite** of brain integration.

Chapter 1 began with the very important ingredient of Clarity in the recipe for dating success. This chapter will focus on Clarity vs. Rigidity and mistakes made when falling onto the Riverbank of Rigidity.

In dating, we can have too many expectations (Rigidity) or too few (Chaos). We have to have that Goldilocks "just right" sweet spot. There are many factors to keep in mind with dating, and only those people with common sense and a thick skin are going to understand how to navigate the entire gamut of factors. Some examples of important factors include your age, the age of your potential partner, your weight, whether or not you have children or want children, your race, your financial situation, or your physical or mental health history. Some people care so much about certain factors that they will immediately ghost you (**rude**) if they find out. (No wonder people start the dating process lying if they have gotten such terrible results in the beginning being honest.)

One example of a dating factor is cancer survivors

who have trouble finding partners early on in the dating process. One survivor writes:

> *I finished treatment 4 years ago and still haven't managed to find an accepting guy. 3 weeks ago I had been on a few dates with a guy, and I had to tell him about it because I was going to be in the newspaper the next day talking about my cancer, so I thought I better tell him before he reads it in the paper. I said 'Oh so I'm going to be in the paper tomorrow. It's because I'm doing this fundraising for breast cancer, because I had breast cancer 4.5 years ago.' I got a blank face at that. I said 'well I had chemo, radiation and surgery, and I'm fine now.' He said thanks for telling him, and a few minutes later he asked if I wanted to do something tomorrow. I said sure, I'll message you in the morning. When I texted him, he said could we take a rain check because he had a headache. I said sure, fine, hope you feel better. And I never heard from him again.*

Dates often drop cancer survivors out of fear, so some resort to going to websites like CancerMatch or Prescription4Love.

The million-dollar question is, "Is the person dumping you out of Rigidity or Clarity?" This is why I started the book advising you to have Clarity (although I did find that clarity came over time as I learned what traits or factors were most important to me). I talk about the River of Brain Integration because you flow down it continuously and your relationship(s) either travel with you through time or do not. You must know yourself inside and know what kind of people and interactions you are seeking. This is represented by this idea of a flowing journey of insight and self-realization.

This chapter explores how can you tell the difference between your being too Rigid (picky) vs. having Clarity and dreaming big. Certainly, knowing that self-understanding develops over time is one way that we can loosen up our expectations for others in the dating scene. If you aren't sure about Who You Are, how can you be sure about

Whom You Want as a partner? See the target exercise below to assist with Clarity.

TARGET EXERCISE

Draw one circle in the middle of the paper, and then draw two bigger circles around that circle (it will look like a target). In the innermost circle, write out what you will not compromise on with your future life partner. In the second innermost circle, write those things that are basically no compromise, but in the right set of circumstances might be changed. In the outermost circle, write the things you want in a partner but which could be there or not in the end with the right match. Sometimes this exercise is easier if you make a list of everything you want in a partner, and then put those things in the appropriate circle.

Once you have your target drawing, you can refer back to it when you are unsure about whether to continue dating a certain person. This is another reason to have a coach who knows your values and what you are truly seeking, so they can assist in the screening process if you hit a nasty speed bump. A big mistake that I see singles make is not successfully screening people within a reasonable timeframe. For example, someone might stay in a relationship for three years when they knew within six months that there were non-negotiables there. There's a reason they say, "Love is blind."

As I said earlier, there are times when our own Rigidity feels like Clarity and gets in the way. I was this way after my husband died, and I specifically wanted someone who would take me to new, exciting places sexually. That was the innermost circle of my target.

Looking back, I felt shame about my preferences, which is a red flag if I had known it. If there is shame, fear, or guilt about your innermost preferences in your target, take the time to think about thinking using your prefrontal cortex and explore those feelings with a counselor. (Make sure you feel safe with the counselor and that they are an expert in what you are discussing with them so you receive good advice.) Exploration with a counselor is useful because you will not experience a total coming together in integration if there is something nagging you. Understanding the appropriate place of your shame, guilt, or fear might help lead to your flowing more peacefully down the River of Sex Integration including not falling onto the Riverbanks of Conservative and Liberal. For me, the shame was an indication that other parts of my personality were not being included in the target I'd created for myself. By over-prioritizing sexuality, I was rigidly under-prioritizing other important values and stuck on the Riverbank of Rigidity.

Now, did I know that I was stuck on Rigidity?

Absolutely not. At that time, I felt like the choices I was making were authentic, but if someone had asked me "Are you happy and fulfilled with your life?" I would have replied, "Yes and no." And I would have made excuses in my head how "life is a compromise" and my life was certainly "good enough."

Life is **way more complicated** than this book's "Rigidity and Chaos vs. perfect River of Integration flow" framework. Neurobiology is also way more complicated and fascinating. The purpose of these simplified neuroscience principles is to have a framework within which to better understand the complexity of your dating life and to help you find ways to piece it together to your liking.

If you suspect you are trending toward the Riverbank of Rigidity, explore the question, "What could be going on for me where I feel as though I have Clarity but I am actually in Rigidity?" A short answer for me back then would be, "I have grief." In cases of loss, the brain is temporarily confused trying to make sense of reality with important pieces suddenly missing. Grief is like a forced rewiring of the brain whether we want our brains rewired or not.[xxvi]

Lots of things can make us be in Rigidity. Prior bad dating experiences or bad relationships can make the brain think life or people are just one way. A form of Rigidity occurs when adults are single and interested in having a lover/life partner, but because of "x" reason, they don't make any effort and even avoid social situations where they could meet someone. In their minds, the effort required to meet a new potential partner feels more burdensome than the reward of meeting a good fit. Of course, there are justifiable reasons to give up permanently, and it's likely that a person at that stage is not even reading this book, but my intention is to give scientific reasons for hope.

Dating is about much more than the one-dimensional view of finding the right person like you find the right color and size suit or dress. Besides the Riverbanks of Rigidity and Chaos, I think of other extremes like the Riverbanks of Rage and Compassion and of Hot and Cold. Sometimes we are so angry we can't say a single coherent word. We know that in anger the limbic brain is firing (think: fight, flight, freeze mode) so in that moment we definitely don't have brain integration; our brains aren't physically capable of integrating. Likewise, sometimes we are naïve and offer too much love, understanding, and compassion to people who have not earned our trust. This is like falling onto the Riverbank of Compassion. When we make ourselves financially or sexually vulnerable and overstep our limits, it is likely because we were squarely on the Riverbank of

Compassion.

Sometimes we are passionately involved with fervor (Riverbank of Hot) then become disinterested and detach from our emotions (Riverbank of Cold—the extreme version of which is ghosting). We learn these emotional responses from a broken world that has not been taught good emotional health.

Reading all these extreme emotional responses, you might be wondering, "How can I have a thick skin and keep screening people when repeatedly faced with difficult people?" The real scoop is keeping one's eyes on the prize by keeping deep faith in your dreams. Your faith does not have to shut out or exclude people; you can care about humanity. At the same time, don't waste too much of your time on the people who are not right for you, whether it is friends or dates.

As we journey down the River of Brain Integration

and fall onto the Hot Riverbank or Cold Riverbank or Rage Riverbank or Compassion Riverbank, all our possible responses relate to our upbringing and our physical and mental health (and probably a bunch of other things that I won't mention or this book would get way too long).

Our expectations for ourselves, for our future partner, and for our (likely frustrating) dating journey should aim to be flowing FASTly down the River of Brain Integration. In other words, we need to cultivate equal amounts of flexibility and stability, as well as equal amounts of rage and compassion and equal amounts of hot and cold emotional responses. Ask yourself, "Do I tend to emotionally respond in one form?" Extreme examples of this include cutting yourself off from people, going into a rage, and forgiving people too soon when they have lied or hurt you.

Brain research tells us that cultivating new responses

helps with neurogenesis and neuroplasticity. Strengthening the brain can be as simple as doing a new activity weekly like opening doors with the opposite hand. Seeking to change common rigid patterns that humans inevitably fall into is not only a way to improve your brain functioning, but it also leads to an expanded ability to see and experience the world. Having this same expanded, hopeful approach to dating can keep the experience of dating more like a flowing journey than a frustrating series of ruts or fails.

QUESTIONS

1. Complete the target exercise. Do you feel any shame, fear, or guilt about your innermost circle? If you do, write about the proper place for the feeling(s) in your narrative integration: _____

_____
_____
_____
_____

2. Can you think of something that could be Clarity vs. Rigidity in your dating journey? How do you know whether you have Clarity or Rigidity? _____

_____

_____

_____

_____

3. Write about a significant time when you crashed onto the Riverbank of Rage, Compassion, Hot, Cold, Rigidity, or Chaos. What might you do differently next time? _____

_____

_____

_____

_____

_____

_____

_____

_____

9 UNDERSTANDING THE RIVER AND LETTING GO OF THE PAST

In Chapter 1, I defined Clarity as deciding what your boat is and what you want your future partner to be like. A third aspect to defining Clarity as you steer your boat down the River of Brain Integration is to know your River. The River represents your external environment; some aspects of your environment are under your control, and other aspects are like the current that can pull you along at high speeds. **Whom** you fall in love with can be a bit like the current. A book on dating that implies you are in total control (you steering your boat) is not complete without addressing this more passive, mysterious aspect of love.

River of Brain Integration

A metaphor for the nine domains of integration
which involve the nine functions of the prefrontal cortex

CHAOS

F.A.ST

RIGIDITY

**Flexibility
Adaptability
Stability**

CLARITY

1. Defining Who You Are (boat)
2. Defining what you seek in a partner

RIVER
Your Environment

- A. The part that you can control
- B. The current, the part that you don't control

YOUR ENVIRONMENT: THE RIVER THAT YOU CAN CONTROL

Let's begin by focusing on the aspects of your River that you can control. The websites where you choose to post your profile, what in-person dating events like speed dating or Lock and Key that you attend, the city where you live: these are all examples of your River, or the environment where your love boat floats (or sinks). Other examples of your environment include your bed, your home, your neighborhood, your work environment, the air you breathe, and the water you drink. **All aspects of your environment that you can control are vital.**

Recently, I moved to a condo where I see and hear the Gulf of Mexico from my balcony. I see dolphins and gorgeous sunrises and sunsets. I've always heard that a person's home environment is important but I never fully understood the principle until now. No matter my mood, if I go on the balcony and hear the waves, I'm calmed. I am so much more at peace here than other places where I have lived. From this peace that's derived from my home environment, I find more energy to give to the world.

Find your environmental happiness, with plenty of fresh air and food away from chemical smells and toxic substances. Work your way toward contentment with your job, your mattress, and other important aspects of your environment. The more you find your home, the more you'll feel like home to someone else.

You want your environment to reflect your values. For example, if you are a nature lover, it's better to live somewhere closer to nature than in the middle of a big, noisy city. However, what if you're a nature lover, but all the single guys live in the city? It's confusing. You have to pick between compromising your values and living in a city where there are many more singles or else living in the lovely forest and going to the city for a date once or twice a month.

I think about that quote at the beginning of Chapter 1 about hoping and wishing for love but not waiting for it. The answer to whatever similar dilemma you might have, like loving nature, is do what represents that you are living your life. But also, check that you are taking consistent action to move toward your goal of finding a partner. It's like floating down that balanced River of Brain Integration without falling onto the Riverbank of Self or the Riverbank of Others. Examples of psychological terms for this specific integration include Bowen's differentiation and a lack of this integration called codependency.

Your possessing the long-term, grounded feeling that you are living your life is more important than the specific details of your perfect environment. A red flag that you are on the Riverbank of Others is feeling like a shadow of someone else or like you don't really know Who You

Are because you are always living someone else's life. To find a good match, we must know what we are to match with that other person.

Finally, it's important that the environment that you control be welcoming. If you are most comfortable with chip crumbs everywhere and a dirty bathroom, keep in mind this could be a powerful turn-off to a date. And this same principle applies to caring for your body, your internal environment.

To end this section discussing Who You Are, your environment and the importance of others, I'll end with a quote for contemplation: "The purpose of every relationship is who we become as a result of the other person."[xxvii] What do you want others to become as a result of spending time with you?

LOVE: THE CURRENT OF THE RIVER

Let's say you are flowing down your River of Brain Integration; you have a safe environment, a good job, basically everything seems like it is going well for you, but you feel like you are in a rut. Suddenly you come across someone who is very attractive and fun, one hot night, and it becomes a lusty affair for a week or some months or even a year. Isn't this how love happens sometimes? I mean, it's not all orderly online Skype screening and meeting up for civilized, sometimes disappointing, dates. These types of spontaneous events make us wonder, "Why are we sometimes attracted to people who aren't good for our long-term future?"

I label these unconscious impulses within us, as well as other unexplained phenomena of love, as the current of your River of Brain Integration. I encourage open-minded investigation but not obsession with trying to understand that current.

Earlier in Chapter 8, I mentioned my over-prioritizing lust and under-prioritizing other aspects that I was seeking in a partner as landing me squarely on the Riverbank of Rigidity. In trying to better understand the current, I think about the Byrd's song, "Turn! Turn! Turn! (To Everything There Is a Season)" or Pema Chödrön's quote: "We think that the point is to pass the test or to overcome the problem, but the truth is that things don't really get solved. They come together and they fall apart."

So, I would like to add to my definition of Riverbank of Rigidity Mistakes that love is not so simple or easy to define or understand. I **deeply and passionately loved** these Riverbank of Rigidity experiences and the people I am referencing. Nevertheless, as time passed, my unmet needs came more and more to my awareness, and what was once an adventure of a lifetime became lacking in other dimensions. When I used my prefrontal cortex to talk about my disgruntled feelings, I was unable to find compromise, and those relationships ended.

What happens to our past experiences when the current of our lives moves us forward? We know they live on in our brains whenever our neurons fire and retrace those neural pathways of past people and events. What if you want to meet someone to partner with and have a family, but you are strongly hung up on a lusty affair going nowhere? These are common dilemmas, and my intention in this section is to use the current metaphor to paint a general picture about the mystery of love while also encouraging the power of the prefrontal cortex to think about thinking and decide our future.

Firstly, I would say to look fondly upon your past choices, no matter the excitement and mistakes made. To do this, you must have self-knowing awareness, which is specifically called "autonoetic consciousness" in neurobiology.

Secondly, I recommend compartmentalizing these memories to facilitate moving toward your relationship goals. For example, rename good memories like "Fantasy John" instead of "John" (or whatever name your hot ex has). Creating this new label reminds your brain that while a relationship from your past ended (and for very good reasons), some specific fantasy moments of that relationship are definitely worth recalling in your erotic mind.[xxviii] Renaming them creates a totally different place in your mind in the same way that reading erotica or seeing a happy couple and imaging that for your life creates useful fantasies or dreams you might choose to store and keep alive in your mind.

Once we have stored those good moments and memories from past relationships in a new place in our brains with new labels, I recommend sending well wishes for the ex's future relationship happiness and then sending well wishes for your future relationship happiness too. This puts the past away in its proper place as another way to let your limbic brain, your prefrontal cortex, and your whole body come into integration about your past and your future.

If we harbor intense feelings from events in the past, such as anger or regret, these are stumbling blocks to achieving integration in the present moment. The more integrated we are, the more successfully we can navigate down our River of Brain Integration. If you have practiced the techniques in this book but continue having problems letting go of something or someone, reach out to a skilled therapist and try something new like neurofeedback, EMDR, or a facilitated breathwork session to break through those stuck patterns with new modalities.

It's also useful to hold onto an image or visualization of the future life that you are seeking rather than focusing too much on the past. Visualizing the future is a way of stretching and exercising your brain. In the earlier phases of dating, I recommend rarely or never mentioning past partners to new partners. Of course, there are times when it is useful, such as when the information is being shared as an invitation to improve the current relationship. You might say, "In the past, I found x behavior helpful when I was upset." (You don't actually have to mention that "x behavior" came from a specific ex-partner.)

Why is it important to explore our thoughts about ex-partners? They can be major obstacles to moving toward our relationship goals, and in that sense, dwelling on ex-partners can land us on a riverbank and prevent us from achieving our desired outcome. Likely the vulnerability and familiarity from ex-partners lend themselves to certain digressions, or obsessions, neither of which is usually helpful.

    The main point of this section is to try not to let your life end up looking like Gnash's song, "I Hate U, I Love U." Think about your relationships from your past like a ball and chain around your ankle. Are they dragging behind you like a burden? Or have you let go of your past and transformed those memories into useful tidbits in your mind and instruments in your life tool belt at your waist? Remember you can use your mind to reshape your brain, reframe your past, and create your future. If the **love** current carries you somewhere, use your prefrontal cortex to analyze the situation before you get in too deep and honestly ask yourself, "Is this where I want to go?" We can have animal lust and passion, but we can also use our intelligence to pave a middle path.

QUESTIONS

1. Was there a time when you were swept under by the love current? What happened?_____

   _____
   _____
   _____
   _____
   _____

2. What makes you feel most out of control in dating? How do you deal with feeling powerlessness? _____

   _____
   _____
   _____
   _____
   _____

3. Is there someone or something from your past that you have not forgiven or let go on some level? Write about this and what you can do to release it: _____

   _____
   _____
   _____
   _____

THE NEUROSCIENCE OF DATING

10 DOPAMINE AS THE ENGINE OF YOUR BOAT

Earlier we learned that flexibility, adaptability, and stability assist in making your Clarity boat go fast down the river. Dopamine also helps your boat move faster, although if it's not controlled it can make you crash onto a Riverbank. In the analogy of the river, dopamine is represented by a powerful engine.

THE NEUROSCIENCE OF DATING

Dopamine is a neurotransmitter related to pleasure, motivation and focus. What recent research has revealed is that it spikes right **before** a moment of pleasure (like that first kiss) and is related to the anticipation of pleasure. An additional research finding is that you get more dopamine when you anticipate receiving a reward and **when you don't always obtain it.**[xxix] An everyday example would be children given an M&M the second or third time when they do something positive like a chore. If the child were given an M&M every time he finished a chore, the dopamine would not spike as high and his motivation would decrease as his anticipation decreases.

Perhaps you are wondering, "How does dopamine relate to dating?" Well, part of that answer depends on how you (or your date) use your dopamine engine to steer your boat. Basically, you want to peak your date's interest, so they become interested in who you are.

Most people have had at least one date like this:

> *Part-way through our first (and only) date, the guy I am with gets really serious. He asks me if I know anything about plants, I told him that I know a thing or two about them. He then proceeds to say, "You see, I have this fear. I have a fear of plants, sunflowers really. In fact, all house plants scare me." I asked him to elaborate and he didn't really make a whole lot of sense. I don't believe he was on drugs. But seriously, who the f*** us afraid of a sunflower and since when is a sunflower a houseplant...*

In this example, the woman's dopamine doesn't rise, she's not anticipating anything from her date as he didn't get her interested in him.

The same strategy applies whether it is your first or ninety-ninth date. You want to try new and creative activities together as a couple, this is good for increasing neurogenesis and neuroplasticity and for peaking the couple's interest. Riding a roller coaster, watching a heart-quickening movie thriller, or exercising—doing these activities together, produces that wonderful dopamine rush both for the long-term couple or in a budding relationship.

Think of the couple as an entity in and of itself that needs a feeling of secure attachment (the couple securely attached to the world) and those nine functions of the prefrontal cortex. As a couple answer questions like, "How do we coordinate complex decision-making with two brains with insight, empathy, and morality?" and, "Do we have enough linkage and differentiation within the couple so that when we engage with the world we feel securely attached internally in our relationship and externally with others?" As the couple learns to boost each other's dopamine engine they spur each other to flow farther and faster up the river. Establishing and maintaining this dopamine dance of peaking each other's interest is at the heart of a heathy relationship.

There are many dating books with strategies about capturing a man or a woman's heart. For Couple Love to endure, getting your date's dopamine levels to peak means you take a genuine interest in the person, asking questions and learning. Having a sense of curiosity is crucial. Studies show that having a good sense of humor is attractive. Dating strategies can be useful as long as you incorporate them into your identity as a whole, (not engage in strategies that feel wrong). Also, remember that awkward feelings can result when first attempting new relating patterns, so don't let that stop you from trying new habits. If you're interested in dating strategies, go ahead and give them a try because trying something new helps your brain. From a neuroscience perspective, I recommend possibly dropping the strategies if over time the strategy cannot seem to meld into your total identity.

DOPAMINE AND PORN

An interesting question that I've been asked is "What happens to someone's dopamine levels at real person dates if they watch and masturbate to porn multiple times every day?" Studies show that the more porn someone watches, the more they need novelty to keep getting those increasing spikes of dopamine. The idea is that since porn is readily available, the novelty of it is gone and thus newer, more extreme acts must be watched to cause increased dopamine.[xxx]

Just to be clear, porn in this case is not addictive in the way cocaine is addictive. Porn is an external cue for the person to decide what it means. A hundred people could watch a porn video and you might very well have a hundred different sexual and emotional responses. If a hundred people were injected with cocaine, they would all be drugged. What happens to the individual who has sexual compulsivity, like in this example watching porn many times each day, is they come to know their extreme life as normal and they won't continue to get the same dopamine spike. This leads to the desire for increasing mystery, increasing risk, increasing novelty to maintain that dopamine spike.

So, to answer the question, the person who watches porn and masturbates many times each day, this person on a date is not going to get the same dopamine spikes as they do in their porn fantasy life. Their dopamine engine causes them to crash onto the Riverbank of Rigidity. They rigidly need **one specific thing** to spike their dopamine levels, in the above case it's porn but you can imagine how this plays out in gambling, eating, and many other forms.

If that porn lover wants a relationship and their dopamine-inspired motivation to date is stunted, the recommendation here is to stop the porn stimuli so that dopamine levels can normalize (they'll do this on their own in a few months).[xxxi] The more the dopamine levels normalize, the more the anticipation of sex, like on the first date, will be a powerful motivator and turn-on.

Sometimes watching porn is easier and safer for someone; as stated earlier, dating is stressful, and requires self-esteem and social skills. If you know anyone who is isolated and struggling, not just with dating, but struggling to integrate with the world around them, remember and apply these neuroscience principles. Encourage them to try new experiences, to seek out and find a securely-attached relationship, even a counselor to start with to reduce the isolation.

To be clear, the author isn't taking an anti-porn stance. Lots of people enjoy watching porn and also get dopamine spikes while dating. Although, that amazing healing that comes from Couple Love can never happen if a person remains single and fulfilled by electronic screens.

How ironic is it that online dating requires frequent staring at an electronic screen? No wonder someone might prefer a known response of pleasure by watching porn compared to delving into the vulnerability and uncertainty of dating.

QUESTIONS

1. What peaks your interest when you're on a date? ___
   _____
   _____
   _____

2. Have you ever grown bored in a relationship? What do you think was happening to your levels of dopamine?_____
   _____
   _____

3. What can you do at your next date to spike someone's interest and rev their dopamine engine? _

_____

_____

_____

_____

_____

_____

4. Write about a time when you or someone you knew had this pattern of needing increasing amounts of excitement or novelty to get their dopamine fix. How did you/the person realize and break free from pattern?_____

_____

_____

_____

_____

_____

_____

_____

_____

_____

_____

11 WHY YOU ARE ALIVE

I just heard a terrible story about an eighteen-year-old who went to an ER in Tampa Bay with vomiting from pancreatitis and was accidentally killed by a central line insertion gone wrong. What is saddest about the story is how the hospital treated the family, not telling them their error (much less apologizing), and suspiciously wanting to ship the body for a private autopsy in Orlando, as if there were not local places in Tampa.

I have been on crutches with pain since a surfing accident nearly three years ago. My treatment has included foot surgery (without abatement of symptoms post-surgery, so likely an unnecessary surgery), a subsequent diagnosis of nerve issues coming from my back, aggressive physical therapy for eight months, and a plethora of other treatments. Recently, I had a back x-ray done that revealed a rare congenital issue that is fixable. **Out of all the "experts" I saw, no one ever thought to order the correct test.** When I look up the condition that I have, called Bertolotti's Syndrome, there are cases of young women on pain medications for **eight years** before the congenital issue was found and treated.

Now, you're probably wondering, "Why is the author recounting these medical stories in a book on dating?" Dating is not unlike our expectations for medical care. We envision **cutting-edge, safe technology** in the hospital (and imagine this for online dating apps too) and life-saving, **mind-blowing events** by doctors (and have similar ideas like magically finding our "prince/princess charming" one day). At times our Chaotic expectations (meaning they are sometimes unrealistic) crash into a Rigid, broken system. (This is another example of how the Riverbanks of Chaos/Rigidity can be found in myriad ways in society, reflecting whether or not that person or system is healthy and integrated.)

It is like this with dating. When you reveal personal information about yourself online, post pictures, meet new people, and become intimate, you are making yourself vulnerable and taking risks in a broken world (possibly more risks than you realize). The techniques in this book will help you better calculate these risks and use your prefrontal cortex, going in with open eyes, protected, and knowledgeable.

Like my foot/back pain experience and that of the eighteen-year-old, we live in a broken world with imperfect humans frequently called "experts." In dating and medicine, outcomes can sometimes be amazing but other times absolutely terrible. You want your dates to be the good experts, not criminals! You are bombarded with less-than-ideal situations and less-than-ideal advice on a daily basis. Given the modern romance that makes up the world, here are some more protective measures to take:

1. Don't **only** see the roses and fail to see the thorns. Think about people as hearts surrounded by a thick coating, such as a box of wood. When you go out on a date or even Skype-date with someone for the first time, know that you are encountering their box. Know that even though they have this beautiful beating heart inside, you

need to understand their box, and that they will be so embarrassed by the dents in it (or else so cunning and manipulative) that they will not tell you things. You must investigate the scratches and dents that you see. This is your responsibility in the dating world. To do less is to devalue your self-worth by wasting your precious time, energy, and resources. You came here to contribute powerful, worthwhile, and loving things. For this reason, it's important to minimize and cut out time-wasters.

2. Some people will see the thorns and not the roses, being understandably hard-hearted because of bad things that have already happened to them. Fear or apathy will prevent them from risking being hurt in love again. If you meet

someone like this in dating, it is OK to give them some time to blossom. But if they don't want to open, don't spend too much time trying.

3. Having your heart too closed is like the Riverbank of Rigidity, and being too open is like the Riverbank of Chaos. Wherever you find yourself in dating, as you float down your River of Brain Integration, stretch yourself to be different. Do your best to safely explore the diversity and beauty of this world. Why else did you come here but to explore and try?

Earlier I mentioned how Clarity comes over time. This was true for coming to understand my medical condition. Friends suggested supplements to me (Side note: CardiacMiracle.com is incredibly helpful for reducing pain;

it's the only natural supplement that ever consistently stopped my pain) and said things like "eat more coconut oil" and "a good chiropractor will help." These things were coming from well-intentioned people, but the truth was that I needed the **correct diagnosis. In your dating journey, you need to meet the correct person**.

I wrote this book to help you efficiently meet this person. So, for the recipe for finding that person, see the following Love Equation, which includes having Clarity, applying this book's dating tips, and that things happen with right timing.

One month before the congenital issue for my back was discovered, the front-desk woman at my physician's office asked, "Are you **ever** going to get off those crutches?" To which I replied very confidently, "Yes, yes I **am** going to get off these one day."

Having a clear vision for your future (Clarity) is the secret ingredient to dating success. Envision what you hope for, believe it is possible, and take steps

every day to get there.

I made hundreds of phone calls, begged for authorizations, did everything I possibly could **until I found a medical answer**. I suggest this same attitude with dating.

When the timing was right and the recipe concocted, including the skills and attitudes described in this book, I was able to find love. I found pure, wholesome love, the kind of love that has healed me and healed my partner and will bring countless good things to the world. Healing and future good outcomes are evidence of **the limitless power of Couple Love**.

Let me explain Couple Love or Couple Enlightenment. When you are not fulfilled in your life, like when you eat empty calories, you always need the next junk pizza. Similarly, if you have a primary relationship that lacks attuned communication, empathy, and more, you will continue to crave other things to fulfill and fill you.[xxxii]

In modern research, our social relationships and empathic communication are becoming more recognized as invaluable food. One example is a study where adults who drop all their social groups at retirement have a 12 percent increased risk of mortality.[xxxiii] **The nourishment that can come from Couple Love cannot be over-stated or explained well enough in this book.** It is mentioned here with emphasis so that the reader can understand **Couple Love is an incredibly worthwhile thing** to search for and even more special to find. The couple becomes a love generator that can heal people, society, and the planet.

In neurobiological terms, Dr. Siegel describes what happens in Couple Love:

> *"Empathy within a relationship promotes improved immune function and a deep sense of well-being. When your subjective experience is seen and respected, and you receive communication of that attunement, then you and the other*

person become connected as two differentiated individuals becoming linked. This interpersonal integration raises each individual's state of integration, which feels good and is good for you. You achieve, in complexity science terms, a higher state of integration than either person alone could achieve. This is the notion of the whole being greater than the sum of its parts."[xxxiv]

Keep in mind the awesomeness of Couple Love, be determined when seeking a significant other, and remember the mysterious current of your river. When I shake my head back and forth, asking myself, "Why?! Why didn't the back x-ray get ordered for over two years?" I think about how my immobility gave me time to write this book.

Here are the messages that I want to share: **everything comes in the proper time,** and **with hard work and the intention for a good outcome, positive results (eventually) come.** I must add that the positive outcome can be **different** from expected, hence the need for STable adherence to your Clarity while also possessing Flexibility and Adaptability with the data you come across as you pursue your goal. This flexibility, adaptability, and stability will help you FASTly flow down your River and will help you achieve dating success.

QUESTIONS

1. Has something bad happened to you before that makes you scared about dating? Write about what happened and your fears here: _____

   _____
   _____
   _____
   _____
   _____
   _____
   _____

2. Do you tend to be too trusting or not trusting enough? Do you think this is good? Why or why

not? If you wish you were different about your level of trust of others, what is one thing that you can do to help change how you are?_____

_____
_____
_____
_____
_____
_____
_____
_____

3. Why are you here on Earth? How does finding a partner fit into your purpose or dreams?_____

_____
_____
_____
_____
_____
_____
_____
_____
_____

4. When you read that "Everything comes in the proper time," how did that make you feel? Do you agree or disagree, and why? Do you believe in your dream that you will find the correct partner for you? Why or why not? _____

_____
_____
_____
_____
_____
_____
_____
_____
_____
_____
_____
_____
_____
_____
_____
_____
_____

11 BRINGING IT ALL TOGETHER

"To love and be loved is to feel the sun from both sides."
–David Viscott

Every time we meet people, we change and we are changed. Some people show us how we like our learned, pre-programmed patterns, how we want **certain** people or **certain** foods, or **certain** locations **only**. Other people are like uncharted universes; you look into them, and their story does not end. The endless creativity available to us through dating can easily be forgotten amidst the hundreds of e-mails, social media posts, and texts we read each day, not to mention the disappointments and lies we encounter.

I hope that I have taught some neuroscience principles and how to apply them in dating. I will end this book by encouraging you to use these same principles not only in how you approach dating, but also in your worldview and as you assess the meaning of life and the meaning of your life. If we can avoid being too rigid or too chaotic in our relationships, we float down a river while sending and receiving love. Our journey down this river is uniquely our own, yet something about it connects to the wider sphere of what it means to be human. Cultivating loving relationships is not just applicable to a small sphere related to the world of dating, but rather it enters into every moment that we experience life.

GLOSSARY

1. **Nine functions of the prefrontal cortex**—each function is defined #2 - #10 below, together these functions "serve to connect the body proper, brainstem, limbic area, cortex, and input from other people...All these functions are outcome measures for mindfulness practice and all except intuition serve as outcome measures for secure parent-child attachment."[xxxv]

2. **Empathy**—"The ability to see the world through another person's perspective (cognitive empathy) and to feel another person's feelings (emotional empathy)."[xxxvi]

3. **Insight**—"An inner sense of knowing. Specifically used as one of the middle prefrontal functions that involves self-knowing awareness".[xxxvii]

4. **Response flexibility**—"The ability to respond flexibly and creatively to new or changing conditions instead of responding automatically and reflexively. Mediated by the middle prefrontal cortex, it allows the individual to pause and put a space between impulse and action."[xxxviii]

5. **Emotion regulation** or emotional balance—"The movement of an individual's internal and interpersonal lives such that the states of arousal attain enough intensity so that life has meaning, but not too much arousal for life to become chaotic or too little arousal for life to become rigid and depleted. Emotional balance is one the outcomes of middle prefrontal integration."[xxxix]

6. **Body regulation**—It means to monitor and modify the change of the body across time. [One small example is balancing the two branches of the autonomic nervous system, (sympathetic and parasympathetic) which can go haywire after trauma.]

7. **Morality**—"The capacity to imagine, reason, and enact behaviors on behalf of a larger social good. It may require the ability of an individual to make a mindsight map of 'we.'"[xl]

8. **Intuition**—"A term that denotes the nonlogical knowing that emerges from the processing of the body, especially the parallel distributed processors of the neural networks in the heart and intestines that send their signals upward, through the insula, to regions of the middle prefrontal cortex."[xli]

9. **Attuned communication**—"A quality of integrative relationships in which differences are respected and compassionate connections are cultivated. It also refers to the ways in which internal emotional and bodily states are the focus of attention and are "attuned to," such that they become "seen"… between two individuals."[xlii]

10. **Fear modulation**—"The regulation of fear that may involve inhibitory fibers from the middle prefrontal regions downward to the fear-processing limbic amygdala."[xliii]

11. **Interpersonal resonance**—"The way two or more minds align their states and become mutually influenced by one another."[xliv]

12. **Prefrontal cortex**—"Central to the process of creating meaning and emotion and enabling a flexibility of response,

it sits at the interface between lower regions (brainstem and limbic areas) receiving input from the body and higher regions (the cortex) involved in integrating information."[xlv]

13. **Limbic brain** or limbic regions—"Located in the central part of the brain called the medial temporal lobe, these areas include the amygdala and hippocampus, which coordinate input from the higher cortical regions, with streams of input from the lower brainstem and the bod proper. Limbic structures integrate a wide range of mental processes such as appraisal of meaning, processing of social signals, and the activation of emotion. The limbic area evolved during our mammalian evolution and is thought to be essential for attachment."[xlvi]

14. **Nine domains of integration**—(see chart on pages 27-28) "Specific areas of an individual's life that can be the focus of intervention to promote well-being in the brain, relationships, and mind. Domains of integration include: 1. Consciousness 2. Bilateral 3. Vertical 4. Memory 5. Narrative 6. State 7. Interpersonal 8. Temporal and 9. Transpirational or Identity"[xlvii]

15. **Vertical integration**—Head to toe integration of the nervous system, such as integrating the competing functions between the sympathetic and parasympathetic systems and between the prefrontal cortex, limbic brain, and brainstem.

16. **F.A.ST**—F.lexibility, A.daptability, and ST.ability— **Flexibility** means the ability to switch behavioral response according to the circumstances. **Adaptability** means being able to cope with adversity or danger without succumbing to basic emotions or impaired judgement. **Stability** means maintaining a consistent mood and emotional expression

and being able to not become overly excited in serious situations.

17. **Transpirational integration or identity integration**—An expanded sense of self beyond "me" or "we" leading to a feeling of interconnectedness of all things. It is integrating all 8 domains of integration.

18. **Earned-secure attachment style**—this term is part of the wider "attachment theory" whose definition is "originally postulated by Mary Ainsworth and John Bowlby, it is the conceptual framework that views early relationships between parent and child as highly influential on the child's development of an internal working model of security that is changeable throughout the life span but can have lasting impacts on interpersonal and emotional functioning."[xlviii] The most healthy attachment style is the "secure attachment" whereas other categories of attachment--insecure avoidant, insecure ambivalent, and disorganized--demonstrate signs of dysregulation. An "earned-secure attachment" is when an adult achieves a secure attachment.

19. **Neurogensis and neuroplasticity**—Neurogenesis is the "production of new neurons from neural stem cells" and neuroplasticity is the "overall process with which brain connections are changed by experience."[xlix] Both of these are possible across the lifespan.

20. **Differentiation**—It was used by the author here implying Bowen family systems theory and means, "The ability to be in emotional contact with others yet still autonomous in one's own emotional functioning." (Kerr & Bowen, 1988)

21. **Codependency**—It was used by the author here referring to Beattie's definition, "a codependent person is one who has let another person's behavior affect him or her and who is obsessed with controlling that person's behavior."[l]

22. **Autonoetic consciousness**—a "self-knowing awareness" which "links the remembered past with the lived present and the imagined future."[li]

23. **AASECT**—American Association of Sexuality Educators, Counselors, and Therapists. www.AASECT.org

APPENDIX 1: SELF-ESTEEM RESOURCES

1. *Dance of the Dissident Daughter: A woman's journey from the Christian Tradition to the Sacred Feminine* by Sue Monk Kidd

2. *Revolution from Within: A Book of Self-Esteem* by Gloria Steinem

3. Gloria Steinem on Self-Esteem:
https://www.youtube.com/watch?v=NQxx1WJcaE8

4. *Women and Self Esteem: Understanding and Improving the Way we Feel about Ourselves* by Linda Sanford

TED TALKS

5. Meet Yourself:

https://www.youtube.com/watch?v=uOrzmFUJtrs

6. Disrupting Thinking That You're Ugly:
https://www.ted.com/talks/meaghan_ramsey_why_thinking_you_re_ugly_is_bad_for_you

7. Listening to Shame:

https://www.ted.com/talks/brene_brown_listening_to_shame

APPENDIX 2: SIZE YOUR CONDOM

- There are 3 sizes of condoms
- Use an empty toilet paper roll to determine size:

1. If erection fits in the roll with some room to spare, choose a smaller, snugger, more tailored fit condom. This is best for 35% of men.

2. If there's just enough room, use standard sized condom, best for 50% of men.

3. If it's too tight, use a larger, more generous fit condom, best for 15% of men.

www.thecondomreview.com/pages/find-your-condom-size

APPENDIX 3: SEX RISK SPECTRUM

✓ **Green or NO RISK behaviors include**:

Sexual fantasies, masturbation, mutual masturbation with gloves, massage, holding hands, showering together, using sex toys, hugging and kissing

✓ **Yellow or LOW RISK behaviors include**:

Oral sex or vaginal/anal sex with condoms

✓ **Red or HIGH RISK behaviors include**:

Vaginal/anal sex without condoms, withdrawal (pulling out)

For more links:

http://redlightheidi.com/information-on-stds/

For more details than the above list:
http://www.scarleteen.com/article/bodies/can_i_get_pregnant_or_get_or_pass_on_an_sti_from_that

APPENDIX 4: LUBRICANTS
See original handout here
http://redlightheidi.com/lubricants-organic-glycerin-free/

THE NEUROSCIENCE OF DATING

	WATER BASED LUBRICANTS				SILICONE
	Slippery Stuff	SLiquid Organic Oceanic	Good Clean Love	Pre-Seed	Überlube
Lubrication	👉	👉	👉	👉	👉
Chlorhexidine Free	●	●	●	●	●
Propylene glycol Free	●	●	●	●	●
Glycerin Free	?	●	●	●	●
Paraben Free	●	●	●		●
pH (normal 3.8-4.5)	High (6.8)	High (6.8)	Normal (4.8)	Very High(7.3)	N/A
Nontoxic to mucosal cells	?	●	●	●	?probably good
Retains Lactobacilli	?		●		?probably good
Certified organic		●	●		
Ingredients	De-ionized water, polyoxyethylene, sodium carbomer, phenoxyethanol, *ethylhexylglycerin (synthetic compound derived from grains and plants)	Water, Plant Cellulose, Aloe Vera, Vitamin E, Cyamopsis (Gear Conditioners), Hibiscus Extract, Flaxseed Extract, Alfalfa Extract, Green Tea Extract, Sunflower Extract, Carrageenan, Nori, Wakame, Potassium Sorbate, Citric Acid	Aloe Vera, Leaf Juice, Xanthan Gum, Agar, Potassium Sorbate, Sodium Benzoate, Citric Acid, Natural Flavor	Purified Water, Hydroxyethylcellulose, Pluronic, Sodium Chloride, Sodium Phosphate, Carbomer, Methylparaben, Sodium Hydroxide Arabinogalactan, Potassium Phosphate, Propylparaben	Dimethicone, Dimethiconol, Cyclomethicone, Tocopheryl Acetate (Vit E)
Cost (drugstore.com)	$6.49/ 8 oz	$9.99/ 4 oz	$13.99/ 4oz	$17.99/ 1.4 oz	$28/ 3.4 oz
Comments	*As of Spring 2014, Slippery Stuff has	SLiquid has a wide variety of water based and hybrid	Can be found in WholeFoods	Has sperm-friendly data, can be found in	Silicone lubricants CANNOT be used

Lubricants 101: Dr. Lynn Wang
Updated 5/1/14

Main Line Gynecologic Oncology and Urogynecology/ Tel 610.649.8085
www.mainlinehealth.org

Types of Lubricants

1. **Water based** All-purpose lube, can be used with all condoms and all sex toys. Easy to clean, can dry out quickly (refresh with spray of water)
2. **Silicone based** More slippery than water based lubes, lasts longer, but more expensive and harder to clean.
   Ok for all condoms, NOT to be used with silicone sex toys (may melt them!)
3. **Oil based** Examples: vaseline, crisco, olive, mineral, or vitamin E oil. NOT recommended, because oils can break down latex and polyisoprene condoms. Can leave a coating in the vagina or rectum that traps bacteria and may lead to infections.

Lubricant ingredients that may be problematic/irritants

- **Chlorhexidine** Bacteriocidal preservative found in medical lubricants (ie. Surgilube, KY jelly)
  Found to significantly reduce Lactobacilli, the protective bacteria in women's vaginas.
- **Nonoxynol-9** Spermicide that has been found to increase transmission of HIV, and a known irritant
  CDC (Center for Disease Control) and WHO (World Health Association) do NOT recommend its use for STD prevention.
- **Glycerin** A sugar alcohol used as a preservative, may cause infections, and may be related to cell toxicity. See Osmolality section.
- **Propylene glycol** Slightly sweet tasting preservative found in many lubricants, may be related to cell toxicity. See Osmolality section.
- **Parabens** A weak estrogen, no studies have shown strong link with cancer, but may be concerning to some women. May cause irritation.
- **Oils** Breaks down latex condoms, may be linked to vaginal yeast infections
  Note: Olive oil can be an irritant, small studies found that it BREAKS DOWN skin, instead of healing skin (unlike Sunflower seed oil)
- **Petroleum** Also breaks down latex condoms. May lead to bacterial infections.
- **EDTA** Preservative found to disrupt tissue membranes (ie. ID Glide)
- **Polyquaternium** Polymer suspected to be the cause of increased in vitro HIV replication in a small study(found in some Astroglide products)
- **Menthol** Alcohol used to create "tingling sensation" (ie. KY Tingling Jelly -- no longer available)
- **Capsaicin** Oil of hot chili peppers, also used to "increase arousal"
- **Herbal extracts** Can be an irritant to some women

Reprinted from C&EN (2012), Vol 9015:46-57

APPENDIX 5: SEXUAL HEALTH RESOURCES

Male sexual health recovery website:
http://uandmetime.com/

Female sexual health recovery website:
https://sexualityresources.com/

Websites for sexual health information:
1. http://goaskalice.columbia.edu/
2. Goodvibes.com
3. Scarleteen.com
4. Babeland.com
5. Pureromance.com
6. Drugstore.com
7. Vaginismus.com
8. Advocatesforyouth.org
9. STIs: www.AshaSTD.org
10. RedLightHeidi.com

> ✓ **Advice to clients wanting sexual health information not porn: Google "sexual health and......."**

ABOUT AUTHOR

Heidi Crockett, LCSW, CMC, CSE earned a BA in sociology from Middlebury College and an MSW in social work from the University of Georgia. In addition, she's completed post-graduate training in sexual health from the University of Michigan's School of Social Work.

As an AASECT-Certified Sexuality Educator, Heidi is a psychotherapist and presenter at Hippocrates Health Institute in West Palm Beach, FL. For more information about her professional speaking and coaching services, visit www.RedLightHeidi.com.

INDEX:

[i] This river idea is adapted from Dr. Dan Siegel's river of integration defined by him as "A visual metaphor for the central stream of integration that is harmony and a FACES flow of being flexible, adaptive, coherent, energized, and stable. The two banks outside this flow are of chaos and rigidity." Quote from *Pocket Guide to Interpersonal Neurobiology*, p. 494.

[ii] Referring to the chart on the next page, more detailed definitions for these nine functions of the prefrontal cortex are in the glossary. If you want to better understand the River of Brain Integration or any other neurobiological concept in this book, I recommend *Mindsight* by Dr. Dan Siegel.

[iii] See glossary for the definitions for the nine domains of integration

[iv] Siegel, D. (2010). *Mindsight: the New Science of Personal Transformation*. New York: Random House, 125.

[v] Siegel, D. (2012). *Pocket Guide to Interpersonal Neurobiology: An Integrative Handbook of the Mind*. New York: W. W. Norton & Company, 466.

[vi] Siegel, D. (2010). *Mindsight: the New Science of Personal Transformation*. New York: Random House, 279.

[vii] See reference i above, the F.A.ST metaphor is an adaptation for Siegel's FACES flow.

[viii] Siegel, D. (2010). *Mindsight: the New Science of Personal Transformation*. New York: Random House, 69-71.

[ix] Credit to "bye felipe" at https://www.instagram.com/p/-CRrkXpK0u/?taken-by=byefelipe

[x] I do not recommend Skype because of the security issues. As long as you are okay knowing that your conversation may be heard or recorded somewhere, then you could use Skype solely as a screening tool in the early part of dating.

[xi] Credit to "bye felipe" at https://www.instagram.com/p/_XMyXcpK9R/?taken-by=byefelipe

[xii] Unless you like your feet being licked/worshipped

[xiii] Siegel, D. (2012). *Pocket Guide to Interpersonal Neurobiology: An Integrative Handbook of the Mind*. New York: W. W. Norton & Company, i p.42, ii p.452, iii p. 462, iv p.27, v p.452, vi p.477, vii p.467, viii p.431

[xiv] Suzuki, W. (2015). *Healthy Brain Happy Life*. New York: HarperCollins, 129.

[xv] The term "secure attachment" is part of the wider "attachment theory" whose definition is "originally postulated by Mary Ainsworth and John Bowlby, it is the conceptual framework that views early relationships between parent and child as highly influential on the child's development of an internal working model of security that is changeable throughout the life span but can have lasting impacts on interpersonal and emotional functioning." The most healthy attachment style is the "secure attachment" whereas other categories of attachment--insecure avoidant, insecure ambivalent, and disorganized--demonstrate signs of dysregulation. Quote defining attachment theory comes from Siegel, D. (2012). *Pocket Guide to Interpersonal Neurobiology: An Integrative Handbook of the Mind*. New York: W. W. Norton & Company, 430.

[xvi] Suzuki, W. (2015). *Healthy Brain Happy Life*. New York: HarperCollins, 251.

[xvii] Credit to "bye felipe" at https://www.instagram.com/p/BAD5PFgpK9z/?taken-by=byefelipe

[xviii] Siegel, D. (2017). *Mind: a journey to the heart of being human*. New York: W. W. Norton & Company, 139.

[xix] Credit to "Byefelipe" at https://www.instagram.com/p/BGZ892EJK-B/?taken-by=byefelipe

[xx] Cancer causing chemicals are "Acetaldehyde, Propylene Glycol, and 1,3-Dichloro-2-propanol," as listed from this website http://www.sustainablebabysteps.com/febreze.html

[xxi] From Alzheimer's Association handout here http://www.ocagingservicescollaborative.org/wp-content/uploads/2013/05/Therapeutic-Fibs-and-Creative-Communication-Techniques.pdf

[xxii] Sukel, Kayt. (2012). *This is Your Brain On Sex: The Science Behind the Search for Love*. New York: Simon & Schuster, *20, 27*.

[xxiii] For more detailed information about HIV antibodies see: http://www.goaskalice.columbia.edu/answered-questions/hiv-antibodies-3-or-6-months

[xxiv] Around 70% of new genital infections clear within one year and approximately 90% clear within two years (Ho et al.,1998; Franco et al., 1999)

[xxv] From http://thoughtcatalog.com/heidi-priebe/2015/08/why-good-people-ghost-how-our-current-dating-culture-necessitates-dishonesty/

[xxvi] Based on my experience and what others who have experienced a recent death have told me, I'd say that sometimes grief "turns up the volume" for sexual arousal. It makes sense that in the face of devastating loss (one extreme) the brain and body seek extreme connection and pleasure (another extreme, in stress we often cycle between extremes).

[xxvii] Adapted from "…you are using your relationship with everything to decide what you are becoming." Walsch, N. (1995) *Conversations with God: An Uncommon Dialogue*. New York: Hampton Roads, 126.

[xxviii] If a relationship didn't end for a good reason in your mind, you might be left confused by ambiguous loss. I recommend reading about the mental conflicts that occur for the mind and body when a person is faced with ambiguous loss.

[xxix] From Andrea andrea kuszewski at https://www.datingskillsreview.com/ep-62-neuroscience-of-sex-sexuality-andrea-kuszewski/

[xxx] Ibid

[xxxi] Ibid

[xxxii] For more information on Couple Love/Couple Enlightenment visit http://www.daveoshana.com/

[xxxiii] Quote is from a research study mentioned by Carol Zernial at minute ten in this CaregiverSOS radioshow recording: http://caregiversos.org/hundreds-of-caregiver-tips-with-odell-glenn-jr-march-20-2016/

[xxxiv] P.112 mind

[xxxv] Siegel, D. (2012). *Pocket Guide to Interpersonal Neurobiology: An Integrative Handbook of the Mind*. New York: W. W. Norton & Company, 42.

[xxxvi] Ibid., 452.

[xxxvii] Ibid., 462.

[xxxviii] Ibid., 27.

[xxxix] Ibid., 452.

[xl] Ibid., 477.

[xli]Ibid., 467.
[xlii]Ibid., 431.
[xliii]Ibid., 455.
[xliv]Ibid., 466.
[xlv]Ibid., 491.
[xlvi]Ibid., 469.
[xlvii]Ibid., 371.
[xlviii]Ibid., 430.
[xlix]Ibid., 480.
[l]From http://www.mhankyswoh.org/uploads/files/pdfs/codependency-definition_20130813.pdf
[li]Ibid., 462.